ORCHID JOURNEY
Personal Tracker & Observation Journal

Phalaenopsis
Cattleya
Cymbidium
Miltoniopsis
Dendrobium

ORCHID JOURNEY

* * *

Imprint: Independently published
Cover Art: Amanda June Matthews

* * *

First Edition

Copyright © 2021 by Amanda June Matthews

All rights reserved. The reproduction or utilization of this work in any form is forbidden without the written permission of the author.

ISBN: 9798597994529

Imprint: Independently published

* * *

More information about each orchid can be found on the website
www.orchideria.com
or on the YouTube Channel Orchideria

ORCHID JOURNEY
by Amanda June Matthews

This journal belongs to

_____

Please note that the information cited in this book are given from my perspective in the United States. Some items such as temperatures, are easily translated; where they are given in Fahrenheit, I also included Celsius.

The harder part is seasons. Where I live, in the middle of the Kansas, winter starts a little after November and stretches out until late February or March. Summer is technically June, July, and August, but can go over a few months. This all can vary depending on where you live. In Brazil, seasons are the exact opposite. In fact, it only has 2 seasons: rainy and dry.

North and South also differ (this matters for window placement) but luckily for the best orchid growing—east-facing windows—east and west are still east and west, no matter how far you go.

Taking this into consideration, always translate the seasons and directions accordingly.

INDEX

How To Use This Journal	ii
Getting Started with Your Orchid Collection	1
Wish List	13
Watering	19
Lighting (Indoor)	33
Humidity	49
Potting Media	57
Fertilization	69
Blooming Cycle	87
Phalaenopsis	95
Cattleya	135
Dendrobium	177
Cymbidium	227
Miltoniopsis	269
Orchid Literature & Learning	319
Extra Journal Entries	331
About the Author & More	357

HOW TO USE THIS JOURNAL

"A flower does not think of competing with the flower next to it. It just blooms." – *Zen Shin*

Your new orchid journey will be fascinating! I can say that because I've been right where you are today. You want to start an orchid collection (or already have quite a few orchids), but don't know where or what to do now.

This tracker is designed to help you learn about orchids and track their progress. It's not an excel spreadsheet[1] where you mechanically type in numbers, but it's a guide to help you track your learning along with the orchid's growth.

Only after I started to write down the data from my daily orchid care, I realized how much I'd gained in understanding how orchids grow. The wealth of knowledge that I learned from analyzing those notes made me a better orchid grower.

For this reason, this orchid journal is not a care guide or a specific instruction sheet to each orchid. It's also not a blank notebook page or spreadsheet. Although I've briefly added notes of general items like lighting, watering, fertilizing, misting, and potting media, these are just to be used as references.

---

[1] I didn't give up on the idea of the spreadsheet. On page 359 I have more details about that.

Take the guidelines as a basic rule and change what needs to be adapted to better fit your care and environment. It's your routine and there are ways to work around it without feeling pressured into a task-oriented duty.

My goal in creating this kind of journal is that I'd looked for many diaries, planners, trackers, and other kinds of notebooks, but found nothing that satisfied what I wanted in terms of orchid care. So, I decided to make my own.

At the end of this book, I've also included a place to increase your learning with the incentive of reading more literature, listening to podcasts, going to orchid shows, and adding movies or films that you might find interesting.

Remember, the most important words in this journal are not mine—they're yours.

YOUR ORCHID COLLECTION

"The Japanese say, if the flower is to be beautiful, it must be cultivated."
– *Lester Cole*

Orchids vary in size, shape, fragrance, growing conditions, and almost every other category that you can imagine. With over 9,000 orchid genera that have been scientifically catalogued, each with different species (around 30,000 different species) it's a little hard to know which orchids will grow in our living room.

The truth is not all will.

You're on your way to making an orchid collection and there's so much to discover. My suggestion is to start with five orchids from the most common genera, then see what adapts to your climate and conditions. Then work—multiply—from there.

In this guide, I've included a few of the most common: **Phalaenopsis, Cattleya, Dendrobium, Cymbidium, and Miltoniopsis.** These, of course, are just suggestions.

Some orchids need special conditions to grow successfully: proper lighting, humidity, ventilation, pH of the water, and other variants. These can only be successfully grown in greenhouses and specialized locations. When it comes to picking out orchids to grow indoors though, the list can narrow significantly.

What are the 10 best orchids to grow indoors? **Phalaenopsis, Cattleya, Paphiopedilum, Dendrobium, Cymbidium, Ludisia, Miltoniopsis, Oncidium, Phaius, and Zygopetalums** are the best orchids to grow indoors without many adaptations from the homeowner.

Please note that this chapter is not a full guide to each orchid, just a revised version. I've added a specific chapter to the first 5 orchids, which I'll explain later with more detail.

1) Phalaenopsis (Moth Orchid)

Phalaenopsis are by far the most sold indoor orchids on the market. These make perfect gifts for Mother's Day, Valentines, birthdays, graduations, and other special occasions. They are so common that you can find them in department stores, grocery stores, and supermarkets.

To best accommodate a Phalaenopsis orchid in your living room, you'll need to focus on two things: light and humidity. Chose a window sill that sits in a light location, but doesn't get direct sun. I personally refrain from saying east or west windows, since I don't know what's on the other side of your window or how wide your overhang is. You might put it in an east window and there be absolutely no light whatsoever.

So chose a window that is well-lit but has no direct sunlight pouring through it during the afternoon hours. A couple minutes in the morning sun or late afternoon sun are doable, too. Phalaenopsis love being in well-lit windows, where air flow is constant and its bright light illuminates the environment.

A "controversial" place to keep your orchid is the kitchen window, above the sink. I don't advise it, but there are successful growers who keep them there. As long as you take extra care and don't pour boiling water in the sink where the fervent steam will scar the orchid leaves, then the kitchen window is tolerated. The constant humidity will be appreciated by the orchid.

Tips: Don't keep bananas or ripe oranges near the Phalaenopsis. These fruit (others too, but these are the worst) will excrete a chemical gas called ethylene when they are near ripe. This is extremely toxic to the orchid and it won't bloom.

If you don't want to keep the orchid in the kitchen, and prefer the living room, add a humidity tray under the orchid. Phalaenopsis have a higher humidity preference than most indoor environments provide.

2) Cattleya: Indoors is Perfect for This Orchid

Cattleyas are another orchid that are easily grown indoors. They come from the tropical and subtropical forest in Brazil. These are excellent orchids to attach to trees or place on mounts, since that is their most likely habitat.

The only challenge for Cattleyas is not enough air circulation in your living room. Adapted to grow in windy environments, Cattleyas will develop root rot quickly if there is not air circulation.

To change this, you'll need to keep a low fan on all the time. If you don't want to use a fan, you can place your Cattleya on the patio outside during spring to fall. Just keep it out of direct sunlight, or at most, allow early morning sun. If you live in a hardiness zone of 10 to 12, you're in the perfect spot for an outdoor Cattleya. Otherwise, keep in indoors with a low fan.

Once the fan is on or it is outdoors, your humidity levels will drop. This is a double hit because Cattleyas prefer a lot more humidity than the Phalaenopsis do. A humidity tray just won't cut it, and with the fan on low during both day and night, you'll need to provide a humidifier.

Cattleyas prefer a 40 to 70% humidity range, and most indoor environments are around 33%. It's worse if you work in an airconditioned room.

Tips: lots of new orchid hobbyist will place an orchid in the bathroom thinking that the humidity will benefit the orchid. Please don't do this. The humidity that forms the bathroom is sporadic and inconsistent. It can be the driest place in the house, then all the sudden move to 100% humidity for ten minutes. Then after a while, it drops down to the direst place ever.

This inconsistency will halter the orchid's growth. The same can be said about temperature. Usually, the humidity that is produced in the bathroom is from hot showers, and the temperature ranges are not the best.

The last reason I'm against bathroom orchids is that the lighting is usually not adequate. Most bathrooms stay in the dark unless someone is in there and turns on the light. Unless you have to-die-for bay windows over the sunken tub, most small windows do not provide the lighting that an orchid needs.

In all, bathrooms don't favor most orchids.

Once you've managed humidity and air circulation, your Cattleya will thrive indoors and make your living room all that much brighter.

3) Miltoniopsis: The Indoor Water Lover

The Miltoniopsis Orchids (which look like little pansies) are grown naturally in the higher mountainous regions of the Andes, around Peru, Colombia, Panama, and Ecuador, where it rains almost every single day.

They absolutely love water, and if you want to try your hand at a semi-hydroponic method, then this is your orchid. You could try either full hydroponics or semi, but either way, Miltoniopsis will appreciate the higher water and humidity.

To grow these indoors, you'll have to be very strict about the water. Everything else is pretty easy to maintain, as far as fertilizer, lighting (they don't like much, so keep them in bright shade, less than Phalaenopsis), and potting medium are easy to tend to.

What isn't easy, is the humidity. Watering and humidity are two different things, and Miltoniopsis like them both are very high levels. You'll need to keep a humidity tray and a humidifier, since they thrive at 70% RH. Just because of this factor, Miltoniopsis almost didn't make it onto my indoor list. At 70%, you're risking the wall paper to peel off and the paint to crumble with moisture.

The only way this works indoors is if you keep a humidifier pointed directly at the Miltoniopsis, and place both by the window. This keeps the air circulation high, not letting the high humidity accumulate around the crown and stem.

This is probably the hardest orchid to grow on this list just because of humidity, so start with another one first until you get the general idea of orchid care. Once you've kept an orchid alive (and believe me, don't feel bad if you kill the first couple orchids—it happens. Orchid care is a learning process.) then move onto the Miltoniopsis. Your reward will be a large pansy looking flower.

4) Dendrobium: Indoors Makes these Orchids Thrive

Dendrobiums will be one of the few orchids that will like a window that does get a bit hotter during the day. As I said before, I'm not much on dictating which directional window to choose, but if all windows are the same, pick a south-facing window for your dendrobiums.

The reason for this is dual: they love the hotter climates and temperatures during the day, but need a cool wind or breeze at night to bring the temperatures down.

Most orchids do not tolerate being in sunlight, but Dendrobiums don't mind as long as it's not all day long. During the hottest part of the day, they'll need shade. This is why the south window works best (that is, if you live north of the equator).

Dendrobiums will also need more water and more fertilizer than your other orchids. In fact, just relate Dendrobiums to being greedy and wanting everything: all the sun, all the water, and all the fertilizer. In this sense, you'll need a humidifier for these, too. They'll want higher humidity levels, aiming for 50 to 70% relative humidity (RH). This is a little higher than the other orchids listed, so place the humidifier closer to the Dendrobium.

5) Cymbidium: The least of Indoor Orchids, since they like the Patio

I debated whether to place Cymbidiums on this list, since these orchids have a wonderful time outdoors. From spring to fall, they will do well on a bright porch or patio, as long as they aren't in direct sun for more than two or three hours.

During winter they have to be brought indoors, so that is why they made a spot on my list. Since some Cymbidiums blossom during winter, they make the perfect peaceful place for winter blues.

What you'll want to check for in Cymbidiums is proper water drainage and humidity. As long as water is constantly around these orchids, they'll do well either indoors or outside.

To maintain higher humidity in a drier climate, you'll need to mist the leaves each morning and night, along with the proper watering schedule. In climates that aren't so dry, a daily, morning mist should be sufficient.

-x-x-x-

Those are the first 5 orchids that I've chosen to add to this book. If those aren't of your liking or preference, here are another 5 that are good for starter orchids and easily available in nurseries or online. I will not be focusing in depth on these 5 in this book, but decided to present them with a brief introduction.

-x-x-x-

6) Paphiopedilum: The Indoor Orchid that acts like other houseplants

Paphiopedilums (also called lady slippers or moccasin orchids) are some of the few orchids that are terrestrial. Everything you've learned about potting medium and orchid bark, sphagnum moss, and perlite can be ditched when it comes to Paphiopedilums. Being terrestrial, these orchids act like other houseplants grown in soil.

Except they still are orchids, so don't use houseplant soil.

A good mixture for a potting medium would be four parts bark and one part perlite. This ensure the proper drainage that Paphiopedilums like and also ensure that the roots are always a little moist. You're aiming at a medium that provides great drainage over anything else.

The main concern with Paphiopedilums is watering them enough so they stay moist the entire time. This may mean you'll have to water them more than your Phalaenopsis.

There are two types of Paphiopedilums: a warm-growing type (70° to 80° F or 21° to 26° C during the day) and a cool-growing type (65° to 70° F or 18° to 21° C during the day).

Warm growers are best for indoors, since the cool growers demand daytime temperatures that are cooler than most people are comfortable with. (Nighttime temperatures are similar among both types (55° to 62° F, 12° to 16° C). So when you're browsing Paphiopedilums, chose a variety that is a warm-grower.

7)   Ludisia: A Miniature Orchid Worthy of a Majestic Indoor Throne

What I love about Ludisia (or jewel orchids) is that their leaves are fascinating. Most orchids have leaves that don't call much attention, but Ludisia orchids have beautiful patterns, shapes, intricate designs and just mesmerize me.

The best part: when they flower, they produce tiny, miniature flowers that are just to fall in love with. You have a double winner on this indoor orchid.

Ludisias make the perfect terrarium orchids, too. If you plant them in a terrarium, they keep the colorful vibe up all year round, even without the blossom.

I might advise that these orchids are a little harder to take care of and might need more sophisticated equipment, like lighting, humidifiers and other apparatus.

If you grow African violets, then Ludisia is definitely the orchid you'll want. The growth patterns and environments are extremely similar, not to say the same. If happen to have the winter blues, the Ludisia is a winter bloomer and will be ready for repotting near March (Spring).

And the best part of a Ludisia orchid: it's a terrestrial orchid. Unlike the Paphiopedilum which is also terrestrial, Ludisia actually likes soil. So if you have any leftover potting mix that isn't orchid related, Ludisia adapt perfectly well to soil and garden mixes.

8) Oncidium: The Queen of the Indoor Dancing Ladies

Oncidiums (otherwise known as Dancing Ladies or Tiger Orchids) are a humongous orchid genus. The American Orchid Society has classified and accepted 300 orchids in this genus, and from there, the hybrids branch out. Oncidiums even have an Oncidium Alliance, with over 70 Oncidium genera and these branch into over 1,200 species. For this reason, it's hard to write a specific care guide since they are grown in almost every single type of habitat there is: Brazil, Peru, Andes, Columbia, Hawaii, Florida, and so on... They grow from coastal ranges to the mountains.

What you'll need to do is research the specific orchid species of the Oncidium you're wanting to cultivate and take the care instructions from there. If you're undecided, try the Shery Baby, which has a unique fragrance of chocolate.

(Not recommended if you're on a diet. That's like torture, as I found out. Try working in your home office with chocolate scent circulating the room... Not fun.)

I've decided to write about the Oncidium variconsum (or the veined Oncidium) since this is what my mother grew before I even had the slightest interest in orchids. It's special to me because that's how I remember her, and what drove my initial passion for orchids.

These oncidiums tolerate higher light than most orchids, except they don't like the direct sunlight for too long. As long as your window is extremely light and some sun does get through, your oncidiums will love it.

You will need a higher plant stand for this orchid. It's long flowers spikes and flower down and cascade into the most beautiful yellow spray of flowers I've ever seen. I know I'm biased, but hey... It's just amazing.

For these, you'll also need a humidifier. They like a lot higher humidity than the other orchids do, and need to be repotted sooner also. They don't tolerate broken down media and will be the first to complain. Most orchids can make it two years maybe three without a necessary repot, but not Oncidium variconsum. They like to be repotted as soon as the first signs of decomposing potting medium occurs.

9)   Phaius: The Indoor Giant

Phaius orchids (the most common is Phaius tankervillleae or nun's orchids) are not usually known among new orchid growers, even though they have 43 species and 2 subspecies. I'm not sure why this is, since they are extremely easy to grow. Actually, they are probably the easiest orchids to grow on this list.

They are so easy that if you grow them exactly like your other houseplants, they'll do fine. The only advice on the Phaius orchids is that they don't like misting on their leaves. Other orchids don't mind, and actually like to have an occasional mist to keep the humidity up. Not Phaius. Keep the water twice a week only on the roots during summer and weekly during winter, and you're good to go.

The one downfall of this orchid (is it a downfall? I'm not sure. Maybe not.) is that it grows quite tall. You'll need two to three feet of space to properly store this orchid indoors.

They are terrestrial orchids, so you'll need to follow the same mixture of potting media that your Paphiopedilum and Ludisia grow in.

10) Zygopetalums: The Indoor Mounted Orchid

The last orchid on my list is one that is easily mounted and will thrive better mounted than in a pot. Zygopetalums will not forgive a soggy potting medium, and the roots will be the first to complain.

Their potting medium must have fast drainage, that leads the water in and out of the pot in no time. This is why mounting Zygopetalums are the best way to keep their roots dry between watering.

What you'll want to note about Zygopetalums is that they'll need extra additives in the fertilizer to really take on growth.

These are just the top 10 orchids that can be grown indoors.

If you have already tired these 10, then it's time to start expanding your collection to the next 10 orchids that are excellent for houseplants. These include:

Brassavola,
Catasetum,
Cycnoches,
Encyclia,
Epidendrum,
Lycaste,
Masdevalia,
Phragmipediums
Psychopsis, and
Vanda.

The following pages are for you to elaborate a wish-list and write down orchids that you'd like to add to your collection.

Tracker tip: Add a paper clip on the top corner of the next page, so you can find the wish list easier in the future. Another idea is color-coordinated adhesives, like tabs. Since the pages you'll be writing on are mixed in between the reading pages, paper clips make them easier to access in the future.

ORCHID WISH LIST

```
Genus: _____
Species: _____ Cost: _____
Vendor: _____ S&H: _____

Seedling    Near Blooming Size    Mature Plant    In Bloom
   ☐               ☐                  ☐              ☐
Notes: _____
_____
```

```
Genus: _____
Species: _____ Cost: _____
Vendor: _____ S&H: _____

Seedling    Near Blooming Size    Mature Plant    In Bloom
   ☐               ☐                  ☐              ☐
Notes: _____
_____
```

```
Genus: _____
Species: _____ Cost: _____
Vendor: _____ S&H: _____

Seedling    Near Blooming Size    Mature Plant    In Bloom
   ☐               ☐                  ☐              ☐
Notes: _____
_____
```

ORCHID WISH LIST

Genus: _____

Species: _____ Cost: _____

Vendor: _____ S&H: _____

Seedling   Near Blooming Size   Mature Plant   In Bloom
☐   ☐   ☐   ☐

Notes: _____
_____

Genus: _____

Species: _____ Cost: _____

Vendor: _____ S&H: _____

Seedling   Near Blooming Size   Mature Plant   In Bloom
☐   ☐   ☐   ☐

Notes: _____
_____

Genus: _____

Species: _____ Cost: _____

Vendor: _____ S&H: _____

Seedling   Near Blooming Size   Mature Plant   In Bloom
☐   ☐   ☐   ☐

Notes: _____
_____

ORCHID WISH LIST

Genus: _____

Species: _____ Cost: _____

Vendor: _____ S&H: _____

Seedling ☐   Near Blooming Size ☐   Mature Plant ☐   In Bloom ☐

Notes: _____

Genus: _____

Species: _____ Cost: _____

Vendor: _____ S&H: _____

Seedling ☐   Near Blooming Size ☐   Mature Plant ☐   In Bloom ☐

Notes: _____

Genus: _____

Species: _____ Cost: _____

Vendor: _____ S&H: _____

Seedling ☐   Near Blooming Size ☐   Mature Plant ☐   In Bloom ☐

Notes: _____

ORCHID WISH LIST

Genus: _____

Species: _____ Cost: _____

Vendor: _____ S&H: _____

Seedling   Near Blooming Size   Mature Plant   In Bloom
□   □   □   □

Notes: _____
_____

Genus: _____

Species: _____ Cost: _____

Vendor: _____ S&H: _____

Seedling   Near Blooming Size   Mature Plant   In Bloom
□   □   □   □

Notes: _____
_____

Genus: _____

Species: _____ Cost: _____

Vendor: _____ S&H: _____

Seedling   Near Blooming Size   Mature Plant   In Bloom
□   □   □   □

Notes: _____
_____

ORCHID WISH LIST

Genus: _____

Species: _____ Cost: _____

Vendor: _____ S&H: _____

Seedling ☐   Near Blooming Size ☐   Mature Plant ☐   In Bloom ☐

Notes: _____

Genus: _____

Species: _____ Cost: _____

Vendor: _____ S&H: _____

Seedling ☐   Near Blooming Size ☐   Mature Plant ☐   In Bloom ☐

Notes: _____

Genus: _____

Species: _____ Cost: _____

Vendor: _____ S&H: _____

Seedling ☐   Near Blooming Size ☐   Mature Plant ☐   In Bloom ☐

Notes: _____

ORCHID WISH LIST

Genus: _____

Species: _____ Cost: _____

Vendor: _____ S&H: _____

Seedling   Near Blooming Size   Mature Plant   In Bloom
☐   ☐   ☐   ☐

Notes: _____
_____

Genus: _____

Species: _____ Cost: _____

Vendor: _____ S&H: _____

Seedling   Near Blooming Size   Mature Plant   In Bloom
☐   ☐   ☐   ☐

Notes: _____
_____

Genus: _____

Species: _____ Cost: _____

Vendor: _____ S&H: _____

Seedling   Near Blooming Size   Mature Plant   In Bloom
☐   ☐   ☐   ☐

Notes: _____
_____

WATERING

"To plant a garden is to believe in tomorrow." – *Audrey Hepburn*

One of the first objectives in orchid care is learning how to water your orchid properly. Both overwatering and underwatering are the two main causes of orchid death. When you learn to water your orchid, more than half your battle with orchid care is complete.

The other items that influence blooms and good health, such as light, temperature, humidity, and fertilizer, do not influence the orchid's wellbeing as much as how often and how much water you provide for your orchid.

Several factors will influence how often you should water your orchid: the size of the pot, the type of orchid, the season of the year, the orchid's condition, the potting media it's planted in, and if the orchid undergoes a dormant cycle.

For example, a medium-sized Phalaenopsis orchid planted in a 5-inch pot needs to be watered every 7 to 10 days. Smaller-potted Phalaenopsis such as mini-Phals need a shorter interval in between watering, 3-4 days.

Orchid health is influenced by how much and how often you water. In this chapter, I'm going to focus only on how often you should water you're orchid, not how much. That part is relative.

It's trial and error sometimes, but if you follow these guidelines there is less error. The main thing you need to know is that each person's climate and growing conditions are different, so don't take a general rule and apply that to all your orchids. You have to test and see what works for you and stick to that, independent of what everyone else says.

1. The Type of Orchid (Genera) Depends on How Often You Should Water

Since orchids are such a vast group of flowering plants, with over 760 genera and 28,000 species (growing in every continent except Antarctica) watering will differ for each of these. Some orchids grow in hot, humid rainforest, others will thrive in desert conditions. Some have roots that dangle down into the top layer of moss near waterfalls, others grow in hot savannas with hardly any rain at all.

Most supermarket orchids that sell Phalaenopsis are what we call NOID, which means they have no identification. You won't be able to know much about them since they do not have a species listed. In this case, assume that it comes from where most Phalaenopsis orchids come from, Southeast Asia or Australia. New Guinea and the Philippines are the two major countries where Phalaenopsis grow naturally by the thousands.

If you have a Phalaenopsis orchid, try to find out what species it is. Then you can research the growing conditions of that area and see the elevation, the precipitation index, the temperatures and the yearly climate change. I like to find sites that are not orchid related, such as travel blogs and exchange programs, but instead of reading everything, just focus on temperature, rainfall, humidity, and average annual sunshine.

With this information, you can mimic those conditions (to the best of what is permitted indoors) so your orchid is happy. By happy, I mean it will bloom and produce nice healthy leaves and roots.

For example, on one travel blog, it said,

> "In the Philippines, an archipelago of thousands of islands, the climate is generally tropical maritime, with a relatively cool season from December to February, when the north-east trade winds prevail, and a hot, humid and rainy season from May to November, when the **south-west monsoon** prevails.
>
> Between March and May, before the arrival of the summer monsoon, the temperature increases and reaches the highest levels of the year, especially in the center-north and in the interior of the larger islands: hence, in general the coolest month (or the least hot) is January, while the warmest is May. In the north of Luzon, cool air masses can sometimes arrive from December to March, so much so that at night the temperature can drop to around 12/15 °C (54/59 °F). On the southernmost islands, close to the Equator, temperatures are more stable, and remain high all year round."

In terms of temperature, that is what I follow when I grow my Phals indoors. Since it's not the temperature that I am concerned about in this chapter, keep reading on those climate pages until you get to the relative rainfall. If by chance you find humidity levels, write that down too.

Not all sites have specific information, but keep looking and researching until you understand the climate of where your orchid would live naturally.

I find it's a great tool for future travel plans, too. My goal is to visit a whole bunch of countries where I've researched orchids. It's a great pastime...

That same website added, "Relative humidity in the Philippines is almost always high as well, and makes the heat muggy, at least in the lowlands. Some areas (usually the eastern coast, facing the Philippine Sea), have an equatorial climate, ie rainy throughout the year."

That is the type of information I want.

One thing that is a common denominator in all these countries is that Phalaenopsis orchids always grow near a source of water. That could be a river, a waterfall, a pond, or even a creek. They need high humidity and love water. If given one extreme to choose from, they'd prefer to have their roots a bit wetter than totally dried out for longer periods. In these climates, the average rainfall is plentiful, almost raining every day to every other day.

How does that information translate into how often you should be watering your Phalaenopsis orchid? Since you know (after research) that it will rain almost 208 days out of the year, you have to recreate that indoors.

If you take only that information and disregard the rest, (such as the size of pot, the potting media, relative humidity, and airflow) you will be watering your Phalaenopsis orchid every day or every other day.

The immediate results are clear signs of overwatering: root rot and shriveled leaves. Soon the leaf turns yellows and drops. This happens because the other underlying conditions were overlooked.

Our first step in understanding how often to water your Phalaenopsis orchid is complete, but there is so much more to add to the equation.

2. Potting Medium Influences How Often You Should Water

Go back to the Philippines and observe where this Phalaenopsis orchid lives. It's probably on a tree and its roots are exposed. There is abundant wind flow and hot air currents cause quick evaporation of any excess water that the rain brought.

Now, look at your pot. If it's a supermarket orchid, it's probably potted in a brownie-like media that was designed for watering with ice cubes. This material was specifically made to absorb more water since ice cubes melt and trickle-down at a slower rate than the watering in the sink does. In essence, the potting media is absorbing more water than the orchid would in nature.

When you take this aspect into consideration, it means you can do two things: 1) space out the watering, or 2) mount your orchid on a cork slab to imitate its natural growing conditions.

On a slab or any other mounting material, the orchid will need to be watered more frequently. Since they dry out more quickly, you can (and should) water them every other day or mist them every day.

If you are not into mounting orchids, then you'll need to space out the watering a few days until the roots dry out. Depending on your potting material, this time is shorter or longer. Below is small graph, but this is what I found out to be true in my conditions.

Not all the information will be true to your conditions, so again, please don't take this as a rule, but a very forgiving guideline. Also, the guide below is for a medium-sized Phalaenopsis orchid, not for other genera, nor for mini-Phals.

> Sphagnum Moss – 6 days
> Orchid Bark – 8-9 days
> Charcoal – 3 days
> Mixture of the Above – 12 days

After the blooms have fallen off, you'll need to repot the orchid in a potting medium that is better quality than the store-bought one you received it in. Only once in my life, have I bought a grocery store orchid and it came in bark. I was pleasantly surprised. Usually, it's the brownie-like mixture made of a mixture of peat moss and other ingredients. Take all that off and repot.

Step two about answering how often to water your Phalaenopsis orchid is to understand your media. If you are curious and have the time, take out a cup full of orchid bark (or whatever media you are testing) and keep it submerged underwater for one day. Then let it dry out on your orchid shelf or by the window sill and note how long it takes to dry out completely. This is necessary to hydrate the orchid bark, since it has been in a bag for a long period of time and will absorb more than normally.

The next part of the experiment is how long it takes to dry out when only two cups of water are added to it. I say 2 cups, but test how much water you'd be adding to your normal routine. Then note how long that the potting media takes to dry out.

Tracker tip: On page 30, you will see the pages to write this down. Add the size of the pot, how often you water, how much water you use, and how long it takes to dry out (by coloring the boxes).

What you are trying to achieve with this experiment is to understand how your potting media reacts to your environment. Since the orchid roots will absorb the water (not all, but a lot) you'll need to shorten the amount of time during the numbers of days you wrote down.

Imagine 2 orchids. The first one is a mini-Phalaenopsis orchid planted in pure sphagnum moss. I have to water it every three or four days. The second orchid is a massive Phalaenopsis orchid planted in a 6-inch pot, with a mixture of sphagnum moss, charcoal, perlite, and orchid bark. I have to water it every ten days. The media is the main influence in these orchids, but also is the size of the pot, which is my next point.

3. The Size of The Pot Influences How Often You Water

Phalaenopsis orchids planted in smaller pots will have less potting media that absorbs water and therefore dry out quicker. Larger Phalaenopsis orchids have more places for water to adhere and more material for the water to be absorbed into, so they will retain more humidity. They dry out at a slower rate, which means you need to water with a longer drying out period.

The size of the pot directly influences how often you should be watering your Phalaenopsis orchid. The material also is important, since terracotta pots will absorb more water than the plastic slotted ones will.

For example, I have a mini-Phal planted in a 2-inch (5 cm) pot, and a larger Phalaenopsis orchid, planted in a 8-inch (20 cm) pot. The airflow will quickly pass through the mini-pot, and it will dry out quicker. The amount of time the water evaporates from the middle of the 6-inch pot is quadrupled, making the middle of the pot always soggy and wet. If you have a fan on constantly, that helps. Phalaenopsis like humid climates, not soggy, swampy ones.

This is where the problems with overwatering are a real pain.

Even though the top of the potting media will be dry, maybe even crunchy, with a bigger pot that doesn't mean that the middle will also be dry. In most cases, it isn't. To properly evaluate if a bigger potted orchid is dry, you'll need to insert a bamboo skewer (or any other type of soft wood like chopsticks, popsicle, or barbecue kebabs) down into the middle of your orchid pot. If it comes out wet, don't water yet. Wait another day.

You can also move the top inch of potting media and use your finger. Swipe your finger across the potting media an inch (2.5 cm) in the media and see if it comes out dirty. If yes, don't water. The humidity makes the bark and the charcoal easier to transfer to your fingertip. If your finger is dry, then you can water.

4. Your Orchids Health Determines How Often It Should be Watered

Dehydrated orchids and orchids in intense recovery will need more water than normal orchids. They actually need more humidity than the water itself, but water is also increased for unhealthy orchids.

Water has always had a way of curing the body, and plants are no exception. When you have an orchid that is unhealthy it will need more water. There is a fine line here also into overwatering.

Sometimes you might think that the orchid leaf is dehydrated because of deep veins or grooves in the orchid leaf. You provide more water, yet nothing happens. This is because there is no root system to absorb that water and the Phalaenopsis orchid can't really do anything with the water you provided. If the orchid has healthy roots to absorb the water but is trying to recover from a broken leaf, or a spider mite infestation, then a little more water is better. Increase the amount slightly, but not too much.

There is no point in trying to add more water to an orchid that has no roots, so in this case, you'll need to water less often. Humidity is going to be what saves this orchid, and not the amount or frequency of watering.

5. The Seasons of the Year will Determine How Often You Water

Remember in your original research of the place your orchid grows? Let's use the Phalaenopsis again as our example. There is a monsoon season, where rainfall is daily. Then there are a couple of drier months. This coincides with the winter/summer cycles that we would experience in the United States.

The cooler drier season would be from December to February (which is my winter). During these times I can hold back on watering, where I wouldn't water as much as normal. Don't withdraw all water by any means, as you would an orchid in dormancy, such as the Catasetum or the Dendrobium. Phalaenopsis love water, but during those months, they just love it a little less. From March to May, the monsoons come, and you can water more abundantly.

Phalaenopsis orchids do not have a dormancy cycle, but will recuperate for a few days after producing a flower spike. It is so minimal that you won't need to change anything about your watering schedule. Other orchids would have to undergo more change, since during dormancy they do not want to be watered and any water you provide will just stagnate inside the potting media.

6. Hotter Temperatures Require More Frequent Watering

If you grow orchids indoors, your temperature should be around 70° to 75° F (21° to 23° C) year-round. In this case, you really don't have to worry about adjusting the frequency of your watering schedule according to the temperature outside.

If you can grow their orchids outside, then you'll need to keep an eye out on the temperatures. Higher temperatures promote a quicker evaporation rate, and you'll need to water more frequently.

Lower, cooler temperatures will slow down the evaporation rate and more water will stay trapped inside the potting media. This is important to know. Around autumn, when the temperature starts to drop a bit, be careful that you aren't overwatering. You can add a day or two during the drying out cycle.

Important Tip: Don't Ice Your Orchid

For the love of everything and anything sacred, don't put ice on your orchid. You might say that you've done this a million times and your orchid is fine. I can't tell you how many videos, websites, posts, pages, and podcasts I've witnessed where people give this advice just because it's common.

If anything, rain comes down like hot tea where most orchids live. (Please don't steam your orchid, either.) Use a warm or tepid water—not too hot, not too cold. A little warmer than cooler is actually better.

Water from rain comes fast, drenches the roots, and dries up quickly. This is why you need to run water over your orchid for a whole minute, letting the roots soak up the water. Try not to get the leaves wet when watering, and dry off the leaves immediately. Leaving water near the base of the roots will cause the stem to decay.

To Summarize All that You've Learned About Watering

To know how often you should water your Phalaenopsis orchid, let's take this short walk-through.

First, what size is it?
Small = Water less. Larger = Water more.
Second, what is it potted in?
Pure Sphagnum Moss = Water Less.
Orchid bark = Water More.
Third, do you have good airflow, as a fan that runs all day?
Yes = Water more. No= Water Less.
Fourth, is your orchid healthy or dehydrated?
Dehydrated orchids need more frequent watering.
Fifth, is your orchid in winter or in a dormancy cycle?
Yes = Water less.

It's really hard to determine and give you a specific answer about how often you should water your Phalaenopsis orchids. The typical textbook answer is every 7 to 10 days, but that is a "cookie-cutter" answer, one-size-fits-all.

Start with that and observe your orchid. Follow the pages in this chapter and adjust to what fits best in your growing conditions.

In all, I want to reaffirm that you will get this right, no matter how many orchids have drowned or dehydrated before this one. We all are on a learning curve and have tons to learn each day. Just keep trying and you'll soon get the hang of it.

ORCHID JOURNEY

WATERING CYCLE

Potting media will dry out quicker or slower depending on many things, such as surface area, porosity, and water absorption. In the chart below, write down how long it takes to dry out for your specific environment.

Days to Dry Out →

	SUN	MON	TUE	WED	THUR	FRI	SAT
Quantity							

Type of Potting Media

	SUN	MON	TUE	WED	THUR	FRI	SAT
Quantity							

Type of Potting Media

	SUN	MON	TUE	WED	THUR	FRI	SAT
Quantity							

ORCHID JOURNEY

Type of Potting Media

	SUN	MON	TUE	WED	THUR	FRI	SAT

Type of Potting Media

	SUN	MON	TUE	WED	THUR	FRI	SAT

Type of Potting Media

	SUN	MON	TUE	WED	THUR	FRI	SAT

Type of Potting Media

ORCHID JOURNEY

Type of Potting Media

SUN	MON	TUE	WED	THUR	FRI	SAT

Type of Potting Media

SUN	MON	TUE	WED	THUR	FRI	SAT

Type of Potting Media

SUN	MON	TUE	WED	THUR	FRI	SAT

Type of Potting Media

32 - WATERING

LIGHTING

"The flower that follows the sun does so even in cloudy days."

– *Robert Leighton*

There are some orchid light requirements that are hard to fulfill with just a windowsill and have to be supplemented. Growing orchids indoors with grow lights isn't complicated once you know what you're doing. In fact, it's quite easy.

Once I purchased my first household plant, a Boston Fern, I quickly realized a big flaw: my house sits on all the wrong angles to provide sufficient sunlight. None of my windows get adequate sun and growing plants indoors would require some real thought.

Grow lights were the solution.

Since I'm not an electrician, none of my electrical-conduit-processing neurons actually understand all the electrical-conduit processing, so research was mind-picking. With a ton of words about information and terms that I just didn't grasp, I got frustrated—fast.

What light to use? How long to keep the lights on? How far above the orchids? HIg Intensity Orchids? PAR? CRI? Lux? Lumens? Foot Candles?

Worse—once I saw how much they cost, I knew I couldn't mess up.

Led Grow Lights offer a full spectrum of light wavelengths, which best benefit the growth of your orchid. They are the best in my opinion.

Both during vegetative growth/dormancy and during budding/flowering, the orchid receives the maximum amount of light without the added heat, which could cause sunburn and heat stress.

To get to the answer above about orchid light requirements, I had to do tons of research. All I really wanted to know was what light was necessary for my orchids? To answer that, I first had to grasp some basic concepts, which actually helped me understand how to grow orchids indoors easier.

This answer works for me, but my conditions are not the same as other people's. To best choose what orchid grow light you need to purchase, I've provided a detailed explanation of the pros and cons of each one and how to install the lights in your room.

Since orchids grow outside, they receive the full spectrum of sunlight (and other forms of non-visible light.) Light fixture industries saw the potential in developing horticultural products that fulfilled botanist's necessities, and produced bulbs that would satisfy this new consumer.

They made a bulb which recreated only two types of light on the wave spectrum because after many years of study, they realized that these two types influenced the growth of the orchid more than the other colors. Results: a red wave light, which is good for flowering, and a blue wave light, which promoted vegetative growth in the orchids. (I'll explain more on this later.)

Except light in nature doesn't come only in red and blue wave lengths as they had designed. Even though the orchids do develop more under the influence of these two light waves, that doesn't mean they don't use the other "colors".

This is why a full-spectrum light was released a few years later, providing a wider range of light to the indoor plants. The results were fantastic: many orchid enthusiasts and hobbyists raved (in a positive way) about the lights, and flowers bloomed more vibrantly because of them.

Recently, LED lights have replaced both of these. The greatest advantage of LED lights over the first two is the amount of light they produce, but mostly, there's no heat produced. By more efficiently converting electricity into just light and not heat, they're more cost-efficient in the long run.

In the winter, orchids will need 12 to 14 hours of artificial light to fulfill standard orchid light requirements. Starting spring, slowly increase the hours until you reach 14 to 16 hours a day.

You can purchase timers that automatically come on and off, which are really wonderful when you're on vacation.

Photosynthetically Active Radiation (PAR)

All plants get their nutrients by the process of photosynthesis, which mainly is getting light from the sun and with the aid of chlorophyll, transforming carbon dioxide it into energy. It would only be natural to evaluate a lighting system on a ratio of how much light is given in relation to how much photosynthesis a plant can undergo.

Photosynthetically Active Radiation (PAR) is this measurement, which ranges from 400-700 nm (nanometers). To keep it simple, this is the same spectrum of visible light.

Plants have two colors which they grow the best at, red and blue. Remember the light developers above? Well, they got this information and produced that bulb with these two colors.

This spectrum means that when red and blue wave lengths are reaching their leaves, they are producing more energy. Depending on the orchid's natural life cycle, if budding or dormant, the red or blue will have more effect. With this tad bit of information, light industries built the red/blue light.

Red (620-750)
enhances budding and flowering

Blue (450-495)
develops more vegetative growth

If you like art or remember art class form middle school, you'll know that mixing red and blue gives you a purple color. May I rephrase that: a horrific, nausea-inducing purple. There is no way this sick, purplish-blue light is ever making into my home office. Sorry plants. But no—just no. I might be an orchid enthusiast, but I also take pride in home decor.

Kelvin Color Temperatures and CRI

Another concept that is important is the Kelvin scale. We are accustomed to measuring Kelvins for temperature, but this scale is how the temperature changes the color of the light. The same light can be a different color depending on how hot or cold it is.

This notion goes hand-in-hand with CRI (color rendering index) which is the ability of a light to produce the colors authentically. Depending on the light, some colors look a bit different.

Our goal is to imitate sunlight as much as possible in our "dark, dungeon-like" living environments. Ok, maybe not that dark, but indoor light does have a lot to be desired. For a reference, the sun is around 5000K and has a CRI value of 100. The closer you can get to 100 CRI, your orchids will look more natural, since 100 is natural sunlight.

An example: with florescent lights, the maximum you can achieve is around 85 to 90, which is pretty good. Further away from 100, the more unnatural and sicker your orchids will look.

A cool light, leaning more toward the blue spectrum, will range from 5,000 to 6,500 K. Blue light promotes growth in the roots and leaves. The other side of the spectrum promotes flowers and buds, ranging around 2,700 K.

To be safe and fulfill orchid light requirements, pick a Kelvin of around 5,000 and a CRI closer to 100 as possible.

Warm 2700 K
Neutral 4200 K
Cool 6000 K

Foot Candles (fc)

When you grow orchids, knowing what PARs, CRIs, and Kelvins, and other types of electrical jargon that needs to be interpreted does help, but the most important concepts are just two: lumen and foot candles. (Thank goodness!) These basically are: 1) how much light will reach the leaves and 2) at what intensity.

The most accurate way to measure the proper lighting for indoor orchid growing is using foot candles. Foot Candles (fc) is a measurement of how much light can one candle produces in a foot's distance. For example, the sun produces 10,000 fc on a bright summer day. On a rainy day with thick, overhead clouds, only 1,000 fc are reaching the orchid leaves.

Some orchids love bright sun, others prefer shade. When classifying orchids to how much direct sun they like, there are 3 categories:

Low-light orchids require 1200-2000 fc
Medium-light prefer 2000-3000 fc

High-light orchids thrive with 3000 fc

Note: It's easy to mix these numbers up with Kelvins, which are also in the thousands, and usually what light-industries put on the package. Remember, Kelvins are color/temperature measurements. Foot Candles is how much light is given.

For math people: To convert the fc to lumens, 1 fc is equal to 10.764 lux, or 10 lumens per square meter. This is important to know because many orchid growers will market their plants with the foot candles requirements, but lighting industries market their products with lux, or lumens.

Your Orchid Speaks

Kelvin, PAR, CRI, or foot candle… If you're like me, then what's going to dictate the right light is, in fact, your orchid.

In these dense tropical forests, where most Phalaenopsis orchids come from, the light doesn't get past the canopy of the leaves. Filtered light will freckle the sides of tress in the higher altitudes, but the average percentage of light that actually makes it through the leaves and to the soil is only 1%.

That all translated means that it's pretty dark near the forest floor but brightly filtered 2/3 up the tree.

Contrary to popular belief, the soil is extremely poor in nutrients. The nutrition comes through the air, floating from other pollinated flowers, rain-washed bark, and animals who transport minerals and nutrients as they travel on air currents through the tree branches.

Orchids "knew" that if they were going to survive, they'd have to get to the top of trees. They adapted over the years (thousands and thousands of years) to grow on tree bark. They aren't parasites; they don't feed off the tree in any way. They just hold onto the tree for dear life.

Their seeds were made to travel on air currents, floating higher up as the wind took them. Once nestled into a cranny of the tree, orchids started to spread out roots that would tightly cling to the tree trunk.

Phalaenopsis then spread out aerial roots, that are able to grasp nutrients that floated through the air. This way, they wouldn't have to depend on the soil beneath them to survive.

You might be asking how this all pertains to lighting…

Observe the leaves. If they are a deep, dark green color, almost tending toward spinach, then they are in desperate need of more light.

If they are spotting, and turning a bit pinkish-red on the exterior, they could be getting too hot, but just the amount of sun needed. The reddish pigment (which is the orchid's naturally produced sunscreen called anthocyanin) could mean that it's not the orchid light requirement that's off, but that they're low on nutrients or just too cold. Be sure to check those out before you move them to a shadier place.

If they are turning yellowish-green, then they have too much sun and you need to move them as soon as possible. Some high-light orchids do not tolerate as much light as they are marketed too. You need to do your research on specific names to discover how to better care for your orchid.

For example, it's easy to say that all Vandas are high-light orchids. In fact, some species are more medium light, depending on their parents. If you place them in high-light conditions and forget about them, it's likely you'll discover sunburned leaves and overheating problems, which can be irreversible.

Now that the science part is over, let's get on with the information you actually came to get. What light is best for my orchid? In essence, there are 4 types of grow lights you can use:

Fluorescent,
CFL (Compact fluorescent lamps)
HID (High Intensity Discharge) and
LED grow lights

Let's take a look at each one and the pros and cons.

1) The common "idea" light bulb, found in supermarkets and grocery stores.

I have to mention this one just to say don't use it. The orchid light requirements just don't get met. Even though these incandescent lights burn around 2700K, which is great for flowering and budding, but on the downside, produce tons of heat and have to be replace every 3 to 5 months.

Half the energy is wasted by the heat production. You're paying for that heat, too, which does nothing positive for the orchid.

If you have no other option, then try to get a halogen light, which is a better version of the incandescent bulb, producing a third more of the light.

Keep the orchid leaves far away from the plant, so the heat won't produce stress in the leaves. Of course, this lessens the efficiency…

Enough said about this one—just cross it off your list.

2) Compact Fluorescent Lamps (CFL)

If you're just starting out with orchids, or the room you have your orchid in has a well-lit window but you're just wishing to supplement a tad bit, two fluorescent bulbs should be sufficient. If you're renovating your attic or basement into the next modern greenhouse, and there are no windows or natural light, then aim for four bulbs per shelf.

The shelf your orchid collection sits on mustn't be wider than 22 inches, if not the fluorescent bulb will have little effect on the orchid.

Place your orchid right under the light in the center of the shelf, which should be 4 to 12 inches above your orchid.

In general, the closer the better, but allow room for a flower spike. Strictly speaking, if you divide the distance from the light to the top of the orchid by 2, then you quadruple its intensity.

Another way to double the efficiency of your lights, whatever kind you use, is by using a reflector on the backside of the bulb. Light will reflect back onto the orchid, and not be wasted illuminating, well...nothing.

If you decide to go with the fluorescent tubes, note that not a single tube will do the job efficiently. You'll have to mix and match to achieve the right lighting. By oscillating between cool and warm lights, this can be done.

In the past, there were mainly two types you could choose from: the 48-inch 40 watt, or the 96-inch 74 watts. Today you can buy any size and wattage you'd like. You can even combine two categories of lighting, resulting in the High Intensity Fluorescent bulbs, which mainly places you in the category below. For these, you'll need to have a special light fixture, which raises the initial investment.

My recommendation is to go with the normal fluorescent 45 to 60 watts if you have only one or two orchids. If you have a dozen or more, then aim for the 250 w.

PROBLEMS:

These lights don't provide the best lighting for your orchids. They will grow, but not to their full potential. Mixing and matching bulbs is essential. Buy a cool light (4000 K) and next to it install a warm light (2700 K). This works well.

COST:

The cost of fluorescent bulbs is wonderful—at first. After 1.8 years, they need to be replaced completely, since they are working at only 10% of their potential. They do last longer than the regular light bulb, maxing out 5 months, but every two years adds up quickly.

MAINTENANCE:

For maintenance, swipe down the bulbs once a month to remove dust and air particles that accumulate on the surface. Even though we don't see these much, they interfere with how much effective light the orchid is receiving. Regular maintenance is extremely important.

Orchids That Like Fluorescent Bulbs:

Always try natural light first. If you happen to be blessed with sun that pours through your windows, keep these low light orchids out from direct beams. Early morning light and late afternoon light are the best, but never direct sun. If that fails or is insufficient, use the fluorescent lights to compliment these low-light orchids. They are wonderful candidates for artificial light.

Fluorescent lights are perfect for low-light orchids, like Phalaenopsis (Moth orchids,) Paphiopedilum, Militoniopsis (or Pansy orchids) and Nelly Islers. Fluorescents fulfill these orchid light requirements well.

By low-light orchids, I mean orchids that still want abundant, bright light, but not direct sunlight. These more sun-sensitive orchids don't produce enough hormones that protect them from direct sun, and they can be easily prone to sunburn, overheating, and be affected by heat stress. The perfect place for these orchids is in bright shade.

Some orchids don't fit into the low-light orchid requirements, but also sunburn with too much light. These are called the medium-light orchids, which prefer 2,000 to 3,000 fc.

Many Oncidiums, Miltonias (don't confuse the Miltonias with the Militoniopsis mentioned above), Brassia, and a few Dendrobiums can fit into this category. (Most Dendrobiums are high light.)

These medium-light orchids cherish fresh sunlight during early morning and late afternoon, but prefer bright shade if at all possible. A window sill is perfect as long as they don't get direct sun on their leaves for a long period of time.

For artificial lighting, they'll want a lower light, but closer to them. To correctly supply lighting to these, I recommend using a combination of Fluorescent lights, or a High Intensity Fluorescent Light.

3) High Intensity Discharge Lights (HID)

HID lights are specialized in producing the red/blue spectrum that your orchids grow so well in. There can be a few options in how this light works, but the main three are: mercury vapor, high pressure sodium, and metal halide.

PROBLEMS:

There are two problems with these lights though: 1) cost and 2) heat production. They have the advantage over the simple light bulb in that the intensity is far stronger than your average light bulb, but even so…they miss the target PAR and don't hit the full spectrum, lacking on the ends.

Since they're so high intensity, the production of heat raises your energy bill, almost skyrocketing it. Also, the wattage can be a bit too much for your orchid. Even though these lights fulfill the orchid light requirements (but still manage to miss the PAR), they do so way too much. Instead of the four inches away from the orchid like Fluorescent lights, HID need to be further away depending on the wattage.

If you have a 250 W bulb, then keep it about a foot away from your orchid. If it's still too strong, move it to three feet. With the 400 W, three to five feet, and so on… The 1000 W should be almost at ceiling height. If you're not sure which to purchase, go with the 400 W.

COST:

The cost of the bulbs is extremely high. It's true that the higher the wattage, the more you'll save in electrical usage—cost efficient. But it's still not cheap. The overall cost of these lamps is still very high. Besides, you have to change these lights every two years.

Orchids That Like Hids:

The higher intensity lights are more adequate for high-light orchids, which makes sense. What is a high-light orchid? Any orchid that thrives in over 3,000 fc of direct light is a high-light orchid. Vandas, Cattleyas, and Brassavolas are great examples. Dendrobiums can fit into this category, but do some research to see who the parents are and its specific species. Some don't like that much light.

This still doesn't mean these orchids thrive in direct sunlight all day. Don't go to extremes by overfilling the orchid's light requirements. Always feel the leaves to see if they are hot. If yes, move the orchid.

Heat kills orchids—a silent murderer—getting away with so many orchid deaths since not many people address heat issues.

How much light is too much?

There is a simple method that doesn't require math (yeah!) which is pretty accurate. Place your hand in the path from the light to the orchid, about 6 inches above the leaf. Observe the shadow. If you can trace the shadow perfectly, then your light is too strong. Move either your orchid or the light. Test again. If your shadow is traceable but not as sharp, this is ideal for a medium to low-light orchid. If your shadow is just a blur, with fuzzy, undefined outlines, then your light is too weak.

4) Led Grow Lights

LED lights finally are the answer to most indoor problems.

LED lights are available in a variety of light spectrums, dictated by what you want to achieve. Being full spectrum, the

LED Grow Lights fulfill orchid light requirements that other lights couldn't.

The other positive note is that they don't produce heat. No heat whatsoever! You can place your hand on the light fixture and it will be cool to the touch.

Why is this such great news to the orchid hobbyist? Orchids react to heat, producing a hormone that acts like a sunscreen. It's actually a red pigment, and the more sun it's exposed to, the more it produces.

Heat has a similar effect.

If the environment is too hot, the stomata close, shutting off any gas exchange in order to salvage humidity. In summary, the orchid doesn't perform gas exchange if it's too hot. Lights that produce heat will induce cell death.

With no heat being produced by LED lights, you won't need a supplemental fan to cool down the lighting system. Some of the HID lights have built-in fans, which are quite noisy. You will need a continual fan to promote air circulation, but not to lower the temperature of the orchid leaves.

In this chapter, you're only observing the orchid light requirements and preferences. Failure to recognize that orchids have temperature preferences is a mistake.

Even if an orchid likes high or medium light, that may not mean high or medium temperatures. If you have a more cool-temperature orchid, like Pleurothallis or Masdevallia, then LED lights are the best option, since they are high light but low temperature orchids.

How long do LED lights last?

LED Lights last more than a decade and this speaks for itself. With every other option, you'd have to change and replace the bulbs more often.

COST:

For my pocketbook, they're an initial investment of a lot of money but long-term are far more beneficial. They cost less to operate, and by less, the final cost is about 55% less of what a HID would cost. Some articles I've read say up to 75% but I'm skeptical about that. It is overall lower, yes...

PROBLEMS:

How much is this going to cost me? If you're just starting out with orchids, this initial investment will be quite high. Is it worth it? Will you even like growing orchids? What if you fail? I know... I've asked the same questions.

My suggestion is to go with a less expensive light to get the idea of indoor lighting, and slowly replace your lights with LEDs as you get more experience. That way it won't feel like such an impact financially.

GENERAL NOTES

HUMIDITY

"Every flower blooms in its own time." – *Ken Petti*

One of the most important steps (besides watering your orchid) is the level of humidity inside your house. Dryness is always an issue with orchids and humans as well. Itchy, cracked skin, splintering fingernails, static and frizzy hair, high susceptibility to fungal and bacterial infections, and skin irritations all come from not enough water moisture (or vapor) in the air. On the other hand, too much humidity can cause mold growth and respiratory problems. In their own way, orchids have similar issues which I'll discuss below.

Most orchids thrive in a tropical rainforest, where humidity levels oscillate from 50 to 70% during the day. To properly raise these levels of humidity indoors, there are several things you can do:

- install a humidifier in one specific room
- acquire a humidistat or a humidity gauge
- spritz with a misting nozzle or a spray bottle
- use a tray with water
- plant your orchids with more sphagnum moss
- invest in low humidity orchids
- add other houseplants to each room, like bushy ferns

Proper humidity can make you feel cooler in the summer and warmer in the winter. From a strictly building (construction) perspective, an ideal indoor environment is anywhere above 30% humidity during all seasons, but the most comfortable is from 45 to 55%. Both contractors and heating/cooling vendors recommend that the levels don't go over 50%. These levels, on the other hand, are not enough for most orchids.

Is watering the same as providing adequate humidity? In short, no. Indoor orchids will benefit from more frequent watering, but that alone isn't enough if the overall humidity levels are low. Don't be mistaken – you can overwater your orchid's potting mix and cause root rot, yet still have a poorly hydrated and unhealthy orchid in terms of humidity.

Before I talk about humidity, I have to bring up air movement.

The name "epiphyte" already implies that these plants grow in the air, as in contrast to soil. According to definition, "an epiphyte is an organism that grows on the surface of a plant and derives its moisture and nutrients from the air, rain, water (in marine environments) or from debris accumulating around it." Understanding how air circulation works is vital to the maintenance of your plant.

There is no use in having humid but stagnant air. In fact, this will promote bacterial growth more than anything else. To survive the infrequent rainfall, the entire plant has adapted to retaining as much humidity as it can.

Some orchids created pseudobulbs, which retain nutrient-bearing water, and the roots developed an outer layer of sponge-like velamen that soaks up water.

As any other plant that trades off oxygen for carbon dioxide, the orchid "breathes" through its leaves. Seeing that this alone was not enough for proper survival, orchids shoot out aerial roots which expand its potential to captivate the nutrients cascading from the overhead canopy of rainforest leaves.

In this entire interaction of gas exchange, humidity is lost through the pores (stomata—plural, or stoma—singular). When the leaves come into contact with drier air than adequate, they will enter a water-retaining cycle to preserve the water inside their leaves. To do this, they close the stomata (causing one more problem). Now the orchid is not "breathing" in addition to being dried out.

Here is where our real problems start as in a line-up of falling dominos. Once the first falls, everything goes to pot. Let's look at the first fall: toxic gas accumulation. With the tightly packed potting medium, there is little room for air exchange (hence the use of slotted pots, or pots with air holes.) This gathering of unwanted gases is what really causes root rot, not the overwatering itself.

During watering, any available space that's free is filled up temporarily, preventing gas exchange during those periods. If there's not a proper drying out period to permit the roots to breathe again, the gas is trapped inside the roots, raising the percentage of carbon dioxide.

Second domino: the gas build-up will signal to the plant that there's a chemical imbalance. To avoid suffocation, the orchid will automatically release phenols. This is the orchid's response system that attempts to neutralize the toxins that are harming the roots, but phenols do much more damage than the carbon dioxide itself. When phenols come into contact with the roots, they turn brownish-black, which is what we call "root rot."

Third domino: since the carbon dioxide cannot be released into the air, it will interact with the water, forming carbonic acid. This is a poison, as the name implies, and will also decompose not only the roots but the potting medium, too.

For example, buy green spinach or broccoli from the grocery store. Without a bag, place it onto an open shelf in the refrigerator. Keep it there for a few days and see what happens. It shrivels up, loses its vibrant green color, becomes limp and soggy—the same thing happens to the orchid leaves.

How can you achieve sufficient air circulation and humidity?

This is the most important part of the chapter. You've read what the problems are, why the occur, but now it's time to learn how avoid them (or fix them, if they're already a problem).

First, you'll want to know what your humidity ratings are. I suggest investing in an inexpensive humidity gage that you can install next to your orchid. If by any chance you can't find them at local garden shops, try pet stores, usually sold by the reptile tanks and vivariums. They usually run around 10 dollars or less in the USA. There's no need to get a fancy one with thousands of extra readings, unless you want to set up a mini-green house.

Second, use an overhead fan with long paddles to have the air circulating at all times on a low setting, even at night. For higher humidity orchids, you'll need to keep the gentle air flowing at all times. Many people make the mistake of turning off the fan at night. If you have lower humidity-tolerant orchids, you may be able to turn the fan off. Higher humidity orchids prefer a higher air circulation.

If you'd like to invest in smaller fans that direct the air flow directly to your orchid, that's fine too, but not necessary. The only problem with these more compact fans is that they tend to be too strong, not having a low setting.

As long as the air is not making the leaves and flower spike sway with the current, you're good to go. Circulating air that is humid is the secret to successful orchid growing (after of course, all the basics like lighting, potting medium, watering, and fertilization).

The second investment is in a humidifier. If you are in a pinch financially or still just testing the waters, a solution to the humidifier is hang up wet towels in the room that your orchid is in. Unruly and fashion-breaking, yes. Does it work? Also, yes.

In Brazil during the dry season, humidity levels would drop below the Sahara Desert levels, and school would often be canceled. To bear such conditions during the six months without rain, we'd hang up towels during the day and wet them again at night. We'd also keep bowls of water in every room, which evaporated before the next day.

To heighten the levels of humidity around your orchid you can follow these ideas, which are all tested and approved:

Tip 1: Use water trays under the pots. Pour a small layer of gravel, marbles, leca pebbles, lava rocks, or any layer of inorganic material into a shallow tray and fill it with water 2/3 of the way up. Do not let the bottom of the pot come into contact with the water, since it will interfere with the watering cycle, and you want to avoid that.

Refresh the water anytime it becomes low. One, single tray won't do the trick. In fact, it's practically useless to use just one tray. You can test it with the humidity gage. Under every single orchid pot there needs to be a humidity tray. Another solution is to use one humongous tray and place several plants on it, as if it were part of the floral design. Be creative on this one!

Tip 2: Group the plants together. The gas exchange with the bunched-up plants will be better since the humidity coming off one will hydrate the neighboring plant. As birds of a feather nest together, then keep your orchids in a small huddle.

Tip 3: Get other household plants. The more the plants inside, the more the humidity levels rise. Even though there have been many, many articles on the internet (usually not well-researched ones) stating that plants clean the air, it doesn't raise the levels enough to be noticeable.

From a health perspective, as to if it really makes a difference, there must be thousands of plants inside your living room—not the interior decoration I'm particularly looking for. As for humidity, they do an awesome job. My personal favorites are ferns.

Tip 4: Spritz the room with an air nozzle. This is a temporary solution and a very time consuming one, but it works for a little bit. In one study, the initial humidity was 38%, and after heavily spritzing the room with water from a squirt bottle, in one hour, the humidity raised to 44%.

Interesting enough, the study never stated what the levels were 2 hours after this process. In what I know about humidity, it probably went back down to 38%. So, it works, but, not well...

Tip 5: Make sure you use outerpots that are oversized. You might be wondering why, but think about it. The more tightly (or densely) packed medium, the less the roots will be able to breathe.

If you are growing hydroponically, in just water, use a pot that provides air circulation around the roots, more than you think is necessary. If you are using potting medium such as sphagnum moss and bark, don't forcefully press it into the pot, allowing room for air to circulate.

Orchids are beautiful, but those pots... Design esthetics demand we use pots that attractive, delicate, and visually appealing. We slide the Quasimodo-style inner pot with slits snuggly into these "prettier" pots. Please don't do that. Keep the ugly but functional pot, or as this tip indicates, slide it into an oversized pot that does provide air circulation around the inner "horrid" pot.

Tip 6: Use a top layer of sphagnum moss. For this to work, lay a fine layer of moss on top the potting medium, away from the crown of the orchid and the stem. Allow plenty of room for new roots to grow, too. Don't pack it on, but tenderly lay a fine coat of moss. Spritz this once a day. This is not for root health, but for evaporation purposes. The water will evaporate, and since the majority of the stomata are on the underside of the leaf, the water droplets multiply the direct humidity without interfering in the watering cycle.

Tip 7: Create a terrarium feel. With this I mean trapping the humid air into a sealed eco-system, where humidity won't run away. This can be created by putting clear plastic over the orchids, like a covering for a well-pressed suit. Many times, supermarket orchids will come in a clear plastic surrounding the flowers and leaves.

You can set up a shelf of orchids too, with zipped plastic around them. This creates an enclosure. There are some models on the market, but I have found them to be expensive and aesthetically unpleasing. You can make one at home using a clear plastic drop cloth. This is my least favorite idea, since the whole idea is to display your orchids, not hide them. This, of course, is my personal opinion.

Tip 8: Buy a humidifier. Most humidifiers are in the 20 to 40-dollar range. If you decide that you want to keep your orchid well, and the above ideas are time consuming or not just handling the job well, this is an investment that you won't regret. Again, you don't need the fanciest model on the market—any simple room humidifier will do.

GENERAL NOTES

POTTING MEDIA

"Every flower must grow through dirt." – *Laurie Jean Sennott*

With so many varieties of potting mixes, how do you know which one is the right one for your orchid? The main difference between orchids and your other household plants (in terms of potting medium) is that 70% of all orchids (denominated epiphytes) aren't planted in soil or dirt. Their potting mix is exclusive to them, and if you plant them in dirt, they will soon present problems that will lead to their death.

Orchids can be planted in a variety of media or orchid mix like fir bark, sphagnum moss, perlite, charcoal, lava rock, osmunda fiber, coconut fiber, pine bark, and Styrofoam peanuts. Redwood bark is not recommended because of its toxins that can irritate your lungs.

To prepare your own potting mix or choose the right store-bought one is to try to imitate the exact conditions that the orchid grows in nature.

Think back a bit about orchids in their natural habitat. Theses exotic plants don't grow on the ground. Their seeds nest into the bark of high trees, where they find all the right conditions to grow. These conditions are: fixation, humidity, light, temperature, air circulation, and adequate nutrients.

Orchids are more prevalent among tropical and subtropical rainforest, where hot and humid days are usually sparkled with unpredictable rainfall. Humidity is held at a constant high, anywhere around 60 to 80%. The temperature, also high, falls around 15° degrees at night.

Looking for support and fixation, they spread roots outward, some to capture nutrients, others to fixate on the bark. High off the ground and far from soil, orchids rely on the micronutrients floating in the air and condensation rich debris dripping off tree leaves above them.

Their flowers grow toward the light, seeking the fastest, most direct route. Their leaves will shift that way, too. Light is extremely important for the orchid roots, so when picking a potting medium, make sure it's not compacted or so thick, that some light won't penetrate.

Recreate those same conditions in your pot (fixation, humidity, light, temperature, air circulation, feeding, and potting medium) and your orchid will thrive.

1) Fixation: Potting Medium Provides Foundation and Security

The potting mix will need to provide something firm for your orchid to grip and wrap its roots around. Take a look at the moth orchid (Phalaenopsis). The large, thick leaves and long, overpowering flower spike weigh down the orchid—usually in one direction—only relying on a small root system to hold the plant in place.

Without proper security, or at least something to wrap its roots around, your orchid will not bud, bloom, or even produce new leaves. Because the root system needs to grasp something firm, many orchid roots seek to come into contact with the sides of the vase. This creates a feeling of structure and security.

It also explains why the roots are so densely compacted around the outer portion of the pot, rather than in the middle. If you pick up a transparent vase, you'll notice this phenomenon. Believe me, they aren't cramped. They are quite happy this way.

This is also good to note later on when it comes time to insert stakes. Since the roots will extend to the sides of the pot, it's safe to assume the middle of the vase has less roots. Insert your stake near the middle.

Good ideas for hard elements that provide firmness can be:

> gravel,
> lava rock,
> fir bark,
> leca pebbles,
> or even aquarium rocks.

All these have one thing in common: they are sturdy and won't decay. The fir bark is the exception, but it still provides surface for up to 2 years that the roots can adhere to.

2) Texture: Coarse-Grade versus Fine-Grade Potting Mix

The texture of the potting medium is very important. Before you stuff your potting medium with large chunks of charcoal or tree bark, observe the size of the roots. An orchid with smaller roots will prefer small, fine graded medium. An older orchid is more prone to cling to bigger, medium grade-mix. This is a general guide, but you also have to take into the consideration each orchid's species.

Finer grade medium makes it harder for water to run freely through it, creating a damper environment inside the pot. Orchids who love humidity would be more prone to succeed in a finer mix, like oncidiums and miltonias.

3) Providing Mix Provides Adequate Air Circulation

Air circulation is a necessity, even in the potting mix. The source of nutrients for an orchid doesn't come from the ground or soil, but the wind. Orchids, as tree dwellers, realized that it would be unwise to not have roots branching out into the atmosphere to capture these extra minerals.

They adapted to form aerial roots. This is important because not all roots will be growing down into the potting medium. Some roots that the orchid produces will travel parallel to the potting mix.

Do not burry these. They are perfectly happy "doing their thing" above ground.

The potting medium must simulate the freedom of having a wind current or air calculation inside the pot. This is the number one reason soil or dirt is not used. Oxygen, nitrogen, and hydrogen must freely circulate.

A)   Avoid potting mixes that are too compacted.

If you have a substrate that is firmly packed, no air will reach the roots. This can also happen over time, as the natural elements start to decay and mulch together with the weight of gravity pulling the top-heavy plant.

Although the roots like a humid environment, these striking plants need the air to dry them out. Without air, the roots will start to decay, turning dark green then brown, later disintegrating into the potting medium.

B)   Overwatering prevents Air Circulation

A common culprit of providing humidity but no air circulation is sphagnum moss. When dry, as it comes in the bag, it absorbs moisture and withholds its shape well. But get a fist full of wet sphagnum moss and squish it into your hand. It will compress easily and form a tight ball...and it will stay that way.

This tight wad of moss will not let air through it and will decompose more quickly. It will also be the perfect habitat for mold—which you don't want. Yet, this is what happens to sphagnum moss over the course of two years.

New sphagnum moss is excellent at the beginning because of its natural format, allowing ventilation to move through it freely. Yet keep a close eye on it, since it has to be repotted every year to every other year.

Elements that can be added to a pot to promote proper gas exchanges are: perlite or sponge rock, gravel, and bark.

C) Choose a Pot with Plenty Ventilation Holes

Choosing the right pot is essential for proper circulation. Verify if there are side holes, or slats, where air can enter and exit freely. Too many holes can lead to excess dryness—too little, root rot. Both will kill your orchid.

If your orchid is still drying out, then check to see if it is in the path of an air vent from the floor or ceiling. Although orchids love air, this unnatural ventilation (either too hot or too cold and always too dry) doesn't help the orchid. If there are no vents nearby, then repot your orchid with more substrate that retains humidity.

4) Potting Medium Enhances Fertilization

In the rainforest, nutrients and minerals absorbed by aerial roots are varied and well balanced. Other leaves and flowers disperse additional nutrition, which can't be said about the stale air in our living rooms.

A potting medium that absorbs the bi-monthly fertilization but doesn't accumulate salts is preferred. I suggest twice a month, the usual schedule for my orchids, but there's a specific chapter on fertilization so you can find what works for you.

The problem with most potting media is that they absorb everything they come in contact with. They absorb water, but also minerals released from fertilizers. If you happen to fertilize too much, the medium will soak up the chemicals in excess, causing root burn.

The ideal potting medium will be able to absorb the fertilizer, but also allow a free release when washed out and rinsed with water. About once a month, rinse your potting medium after utilizing fertilizer. This washes away the excess fertilizer and avoids salt residue, or salt build-up on the top of the pot.

5)   Potting Mix will Allow Good Water Flow

Drainage, drainage, drainage. The potting mix needs to let the water rinse out quickly. The roots need to be able to have access to the water and when enough is enough, they need a quick exit to be able to breathe again.

If your orchid is taking too long to drain water, then you need to replant it with bigger elements. You can use marbles, aquarium pebbles, lava rocks, or anything that is inorganic and sturdy.

Bigger elements provide a wider surface area, but also, a more direct one. Think of an obstacle course: a straight line with only two larger obstacles is easier and faster to finish than the same line with 15 or 20 smaller obstacles to overcome.

Important Tip: Why water if I mist my orchids?

Misting orchids can be extremely beneficial if done correctly—deathly if done wrong. When misting, water accumulates on the roots, leaves and flower spike. Don't mist near the crown (or stem). Minuscule droplets of water will hydrate and elevate the humidity, but if left to sitting on the leaves for hours on end can cause problems. If you have a good fan that can dry up the water droplet form the mist quickly, then misting is actually the best solution.

6) Humidity: Too Much or Too Little

With a potting medium that holds too much humidity, the tiny white hairy structures on the roots will start to decay. As in any compost pile, the decay will call a party for a mold culture, which in turn, will cause root rot throughout the pot.

Pretty soon, your orchid is dead.

Hard task for the potting mix: to provide just the right amount of humidity so the roots can soak it up, yet let it air out in time to not promote root decay. This is where softer materials come in handy, like sphagnum moss, charcoal, and natural fibers like coconut husks.

Charcoal – An Excellent Addition

Charcoal is an element that works well here. It can absorb some humidity, but not a lot. It's perfect because it also absorbs contaminants in the potting medium and eliminates some of the odors.

I use charcoal in almost all my designs, just to keep the humidity levels constant. It drains well since it's bigger, promoting elimination of harmful bacteria. Not taking into consideration the mess it is to deal with, charcoal only adds positive notes to our floral designs and terrariums.

Natural Fibers, like Coconut Fiber Are Essential

Coconut fibers (husks) and some tree barks are good at absorbing humidity, too, like fir bark. Water will soak into the bark and take a longer time to leave, giving the plant humidity long after you've taken it out of the kitchen sink.

Beware of adding too many coconut fibers. They tend to retain a higher level of salt residue. Before adding them to any potting mix, be sure to rinse them out. It would be better if you can soak them in water from one day to the next. If this is not possible, use hot water to rinse them out thoroughly.

GENUS	DAYS IN BETWEEN WATERING	POTTING MIX
Dendrobium Vanda	3 or less	Coarse-grade
Cattleya	4 to 7	Coarse- to medium-grade, absorbent
Cymbidium Paphiopedilum Phalaenopsis	7	Medium- to fine-grade, highly absorbent

7) Orchid Roots Seek Light

Orchid roots also photosynthesize through chlorophyll. When they are wrapped around a tree, they'll be blessed with constant sunlight, filtered by the trees leaves.

This is the number one reason orchid enthusiast use transparent, plastic potting pots. They are ugly, yes, horrendously so. But their functionality exceeds their beauty and that is why you should use them, too.

As mentioned before, the orchid roots wrap around the sides of the pot naturally sticking to the plastic sides. Light can pass through the clear vase and through good potting medium, giving them another way to provide substance and promote health.

If an orchid is sitting in potting medium that's too compact or doesn't provide space in between the various elements, (translation: the roots don't receive adequate lighting) they'll need more nutrients in the long run.

How to Plant with the Correct Potting Mix

The basics of what and why each element is important to potting medium was covered above. There is one more thing that interferes with potting medium: how to use it.

Number one rule: avoid smashing down the substrate.

To pot your orchids, make a mound in the middle, like a tiny volcano. Place the roots outward, embracing and extending to the sides of the mound, but not touching the sides of the pot. Adding potting mix around the exterior of the roots, up to the crown.

Here is where lighting is important. Don't cram your potting medium down into the exterior sides of the pot. You aren't planting a tree.

The substrate must be firm, but that doesn't mean overly compact. Allow light and ventilation to penetrate the interior of the vase and your orchid will thank you with a gorgeous bloom.

Make Your Own Potting Medium

You can make your own potting medium by selecting the properties that your orchids love to live in, and recreate that.

A) **To make a finer potting mix for your orchid, you need to add:**

- **4-parts fir bark** or fine grade coconut. If you don't have these, you can use husk chips.

- **Add 1-part charcoal**, but make sure it's broken into smaller, finer pieces. To save on money, you can buy the cooking charcoal you use on the grill, just make sure there are no artificial additives (like scents and fire inducing chemicals...). Buy the charcoal with the least number of extra additives possible. After all, you don't want your orchid smelling like smoked bacon.

- Finally add **1-part horticultural-grade perlite**. You can change this for small-grade aliflor (clay pebbles) if you'd like.

B)   To make a Medium Mix for your orchid, you need to add:

Instead of using a fine grade fir bark, use a medium-grade one. Then follow the same recipe as above, maintaining the same proportions as above, 4 to 1 to 1. A medium-grade mix is usually more appreciated by Cattleyas and Phalaenopsis, and more mature/larger orchids, since their roots are bigger.

When is the best time to change the potting medium?

Provide fresh potting medium before you introduce your newly acquired orchid to the rest of your orchid collection. Many people will buy an orchid and as soon as they get home will repot it.

If the orchid is in bloom, my suggestion is to postpone the repot just a bit. Don't repot it now. Wait until the flowers have fallen off and then, after trimming, set out to repot—if you can. Yet, it's best to risk a setback than to contaminate your other orchids with whatever is on your newly acquired orchid.

GENERAL NOTES

GENERAL NOTES

FERTILIZATION

"Don't wait for someone to bring you flowers. Plant your own garden and decorate your own soul." – *Luther Burbank*

Orchids don't thrive on water and sunlight alone. In their natural habitat, orchids receive nutrients from the overhead leaves which form a canopy above them. Nutrients floating in the air fall onto their roots and provide them with extra minerals that keep them healthy.

In our home environments, this is harder to achieve, but can be done using fertilizer.

What's the best fertilizer for orchids?

Depending on the part of the life cycle that your orchid is in, specific nutrients will be necessary in the fertilizer. When the orchid is blossoming, the best fertilizer is one with a high phosphorous ratio, but in less quantity. When the orchid is in active root growth, it will need a fertilizer that is high in phosphorous and potassium. When the orchid is producing flower spikes and new leaves, the top rating orchid fertilizer is one that has a high nitrogen ratio.

As you can see, there is no one specific answer to what the best orchid fertilizer is, since it all depends on different variants.

What is in orchid fertilizer?

Fertilizer for orchids is composed of a three-part number separated by dashes, composed of nitrogen, phosphorous, and potassium. Some fertilizers have a small dose of calcium and magnesium, but most concentrate on the first three elements. This number is called the N-P-K ratio, and is the balance of three nutrients that make up the fertilizer.

Each one will promote a specific quality in your plant, so picking the right one is essential. Before I explain each one, let's look at what fertilizer is and isn't. Knowing how to pick the best fertilizer for orchids is essential to growing orchids.

Basic Orchid Fertilization Information

It is important to note that orchid fertilizer is not a miracle—unlike one brand name suggests. Nutrition doesn't come from fertilizers, but from photosynthesis and

- sun / light
- water
- humidity

Orchid fertilizers will aid in speeding up the natural process of the orchid, inducing the production of chlorophyll, stimulating leaf growth, and aiding in conditions that the orchid already is living in.

One common mistake that new orchid growers have is that fertilizers are used as plant medicines. "Oh, my orchid is yellowish-green. Let's add a fertilizer." Band-aid type treatment is not proper fertilization. In this aspect, use fertilizers to stimulate a healthy plant, not cure a dying one.

Orchid Food or Orchid Fertilizer?

Have you ever heard the term orchid food? What's the difference between orchid food and fertilizer? Orchid fertilizer is not orchid food, since orchids photosynthesize their food from the interaction of chlorophyll and sunlight. The additional minerals and chemicals in fertilizer aid the orchid in the construction of chlorophyll and other important plant structures, facilitating the strength and health of plant cells.

Many producers advertise their fertilizers as food, but what fertilizer does is supply extra minerals that can aid rapid and healthy growth. The fertilizer acts as a supplement to provide additional nutrition to your orchid since in nature it would be receiving much more than we can provide for it in our homes.

That is why it is important to not only fertilize, but also to supply extra minerals like Magnesium, Calcium, and Nitrogen to your orchid. What you could be giving to your orchid may not be enough, independent of which method you use.

Nitrogen in Orchid Fertilizer: Proper Leaf Growth

The first number represents how much nitrogen(N) is in the fertilizer.

Nitrogen is responsible for the rich, luscious green color in the leaves and spike. When used in lawn or plant fertilizers, nitrogen will promote healthy, rich green leaves. If given too much, the plant will forfeit flowers, fruit, and roots, focusing wholly on leaves. If your orchid lacks nitrogen, the leaves might turn a yellowish-green color, in contrast to the vibrant green.

Nitrogen (N) is part of the air we breathe and moves around easily/freely in the potting medium as it does in soil. When watering, nitrogen is usually washed away. The loss of nitrogen is called leaching.

When looking at a bag of orchid fertilizer, you might not see the word nitrogen, but nitrate or ammoniacal nitrogen. Both these are the same—well, for us. Chemistry majors will disagree.

In any case, your orchid needs a fertilizer that contains nitrogen, but not much over the number (which is a percentage) of 20. Stay away from urea nitrogen. I'll explain why later on.

Phosphorous in Orchid Fertilizer: Root Development

The second ingredient is Phosphorus (P) or Phosphate (P_2O_5). Phosphorous will concentrate on the development of healthy roots, seeds, and flowers. Its reproductive cycle is the target, as phosphorus will concentrate on propagating its species.

* I've seen Phosphorus spelled with a U and without, so I decided to please both Trojans and Greeks and use both spellings in this chapter.

If the plant lacks phosphorus, it might become a bit "purply" colored instead of rich, luscious green. Growth will be delayed and stunted, as you compare it to other plants that grow like weeds.

The lack of steady growth is an indication that your orchid is lacking Phosphorus.

Phosphorus, unlike nitrogen which can suffer from leaching, remains in the soil even after hard rains and constant watering. It can become too concentrated quickly.

In high quantities, it's not beneficial for any plant and downright harmful for humans. That is why many states in the USA have issued concerns for fertilizing with phosphorous in large fields, as the rainwater might transmit these high doses and contaminate rivers, streams and other waterways.

Potassium in Orchid Fertilizer: The Natural Defense

The last ingredient in the N-P-K ratio is potassium (K) or potash (K2O). Potassium serves as an overall stimulant for the well-being of the plant, as it helps the orchid fight of pests and disease. Potassium will enhance the orchid's resistance to drought, heat, and cold. This is why we call potassium the natural defense.

It does encourage root growth and also leaf production, but not as much as the first two elements.

Putting the N-P-K Ratio into Practical Terms

Let's put into practice what you already know. Look back to the numbers on the orchid fertilizer label, or the N-P-K. Using an example, let's say it's 5-10-10. That means that the percentage of each item are:

nitrogen is 5%, phosphorous is 10%, potassium is 10%

In practical terms, you'd use this fertilizer when focusing less on leaf production and more on flowering and root stimulation.

Phosphorous and potassium are found in higher quantities in lawn soil, so most fertilizer producers focus on giving the public higher rates of nitrogen.

Orchids will need a fertilizer that has higher levels of both P and K than your local bag of fertilizer.

What's the best N-P-K ratio for orchids?

What most orchid growers aim for is a fertilizer that is "balanced," having a 20-20-20 ratio to it. Whatever fertilizer you do use, you need to find one that is "complete," which means none of the numbers are zero.

Another reminder: if you read the fertilizer and it has traces of urea in it, ditch it. It's not appropriate for your orchid.

You'll notice that not all fertilizers add up to 100%. In fact, none do. For example, even our best fertilizer with a 20-20-20 ratio hits the 60% mark. What's in the other 40%?

There can be an additional number of other macronutrients, such as magnesium, calcium, iron, nickel, sulfur, boron and chlorine. There might be some micronutrients as well, such as copper, carbon, hydrogen, oxygen, and zinc.

Tip: if you look up macronutrients and micronutrients for orchids, you'll find that this list is different than the list of nutrients for humans. Macro and micro are not related to size (in this case) but to what the orchids need in terms of quantity.

How much orchid fertilizer do I use?

This is the tricky part, but keep in mind a minimalist concept: less is more. I'll use the liquid fertilizers as an example, since other formats (crystals, sticks, pellets, etc.) are harder to specify.

If the fertilizer says to dilute two tablespoons in water, then use half a teaspoon. Cut it back to ¼ of what the manufacturer suggests, no matter what the brand. Too much fertilizer is always harmful, but not enough fertilizer will have little to no effect on your orchid.

Why do manufacturers do this?

Well, first, they don't know how big your orchid is. Do you have a massive 10-year-old orchid with several shoots, stems, and flower spikes? Probably not. Your orchid is most likely newer (so it will be a smaller plant) and potted by itself.

Another point to ponder: fertilizer manufacturers want to sell their product. By using up your product in higher quantities, you'll run out faster and have to buy more. So why not suggest to use more than normal? From a strictly financial perspective, they can't go wrong. But you can.

Your orchid will most likely suffer from too much fertilizer. If you use the total amount of fertilizer listed in the instructions, which is way too much in ALL brands, your orchid will start to show signs:

- brown leaves
- root damage
- salt build-up

No matter what the instructions say, use less. You can't go wrong.

In fact, one of the most common complaints among consumers is that their orchids died and the leaves shriveled up after using fertilizer. The usual time for this reaction is two weeks. Even though it's hard to blame a fertilizer alone, the probable cause is too much fertilizer.

But aren't fertilizers good for the plant? Yes.

Except everything in excess is bad. Drink four glasses of water a day is healthy, but drowning in water is not. Neither is drinking two gallons of water. You can actually rinse away the good electrolytes circulating in your body and become very faint and weak.

The same applies to fertilizer. Keep the dosage low—always.

Important: Root Burn Due to Fertilizer

Dry roots are thirsty and avid absorbents. They will more than likely soak up excess quantities of pure orchid fertilizer.

Contrary to popular belief, applying fertilizer directly on dry roots doesn't cause extensive root burn.

In nature, the first dose of water will be with an increased amount of natural fertilizer. Water trickles down off the overhead leaves in the forest canopy, rich with minerals and nutrients. If applying fertilizer on dry roots were a problem, then nature would be the first to burn the orchid roots.

What causes root burn is not the application on dry roots, but the the application of too much fertilizer. Once that first dose of highly fertilized water hits the roots, the amount of nutrient-rich water will decrease.

If you are just starting out, it's better to play it safe and build up confidence in fertilizing. Let the roots refresh themselves with a good dose of water like a quick mist. After they turn into that vibrant green color we all love and adore, then feed them with ¼ of the dose of orchid fertilizer. Once you have that routine down, you can apply fertilized water directly to the dry roots.

Do I fertilize my orchid all year round?

In short, no. During the orchid's life cycle, there are times to increase fertilization and other times to halt it completely.

During growth periods, when you see new leaves appear or a new flower spike shoot out from in between the leaves, upgrade the fertilization. This is the best period to invest in fertilizer and ensure that it has enough nutrients and added minerals to produce new flowers, roots, and stems.

Some producers say that during the active bloom, you don't need to add any more fertilizer. In fact, you can cut it down to half or none. The orchids aren't in a growing stage, no matter what the label on the fertilizer says.

During the flowering stage, I'll use a 10-20-10 that is high in Phosphorous.

When an orchid has flowers, it is concentrating on pollination and reproducing its species. All its efforts will be in attracting pollinators, stunting growth everywhere else. There is no dynamic development in the plant in terms of stem, flower spikes, or new leaves.

You can use the 10-20-10, but use less of what you'd normally use. I'd still fertilize though, since during dormancy you won't.

Don't use orchid fertilizer when the plant is dormant.

It will be practically useless. There won't be any harm done if you do, but you'll be watering your money down the drain.

Some orchids will bloom during summer; others blossom during winter. Summer bloomers will prefer more fertilizer during their winter months than a winter bloomer will. Other lucky species bloom twice a year, so you'll need to keep fertilization constant.

After the flowers fall off and the flower spike drops, most orchids will go into a dormant period. If you decide to cut the spike leaving two or three nodes to induce rebloom, then continue the fertilization, since this will stimulate it to keep producing new growth.

If not, when you cut back the flower spike to the nearest node next to the base, growth will halt and the orchid will go dormant. These next few weeks up to a few months you can use less fertilizer.

Observation: Most Phalaenopsis orchids do not do dormant.

The Best Orchid Fertilizer Methods on the Market

If you do a quick research on Amazon or eBay, you'll see literally thousands of options for orchid fertilizers, ranging anywhere from 3 to 60 dollars. They may be liquids, to which you need to dilute in water. Some can come as misting sprays; others are self-dissolving crystals.

To pick the one that is the right fertilizer for you, you'll need to incorporate fertilization into your weekly routine. It doesn't matter if the fertilizer is a top-notch brand if you simply forget to use it.

Find a method that will easily integrate into your watering cycle, so you can do both activities at the same time.

Tracker Tip: Fill in the dates then color-code the following pages to know when you fertilized last and with what fertilizer. Each supplement should have its own color.

I left the dates blank so you can also write down the name/number of the orchid in the blank if you changed its fertilizer or applied a supplement.

Once you have more orchids, it's best to keep the fertilization simple (balanced works best) and try to find one fertilizer that fits all orchids, only changing this regime when the orchid is in dormancy or is flowering.

This first chart is to keep track of fertilizing in general, assuming you are using a balanced fertilizer. Yet, the beauty of this tracker is that you can make it into what you'd like. You can use it as a watering tracker, too, if you water your orchids at all the same intervals.

The second part (the yearly calendar on pages 84-85) is used when you need to change fertilizers, either increasing the dose or decreasing it. I'll explain more when you get to those pages, but just know that these first pages (79-82) are for overall fertilizing.

– ORCHID JOURNEY –

MONTHLY FERTILIZATION

Fill in the dates and write down when you last fertilized.

January

Sun.	Mon.	Tues.	Wed.	Thurs.	Fri.	Sat.

February

Sun.	Mon.	Tues.	Wed.	Thurs.	Fri.	Sat.

March

Sun.	Mon.	Tues.	Wed.	Thurs.	Fri.	Sat.

MONTHLY FERTILIZATION

Fill in the dates and write down when you last fertilized.

April

Sun.	Mon.	Tues.	Wed.	Thurs.	Fri.	Sat.

May

Sun.	Mon.	Tues.	Wed.	Thurs.	Fri.	Sat.

June

Sun.	Mon.	Tues.	Wed.	Thurs.	Fri.	Sat.

MONTHLY FERTILIZATION

Fill in the dates and write down when you last fertilized.

July

Sun.	Mon.	Tues.	Wed.	Thurs.	Fri.	Sat.

August

Sun.	Mon.	Tues.	Wed.	Thurs.	Fri.	Sat.

September

Sun.	Mon.	Tues.	Wed.	Thurs.	Fri.	Sat.

ORCHID JOURNEY

MONTHLY FERTILIZATION

Fill in the dates and write down when you last fertilized.

October

Sun.	Mon.	Tues.	Wed.	Thurs.	Fri.	Sat.

November

Sun.	Mon.	Tues.	Wed.	Thurs.	Fri.	Sat.

December

Sun.	Mon.	Tues.	Wed.	Thurs.	Fri.	Sat.

FERTILIZER CHART

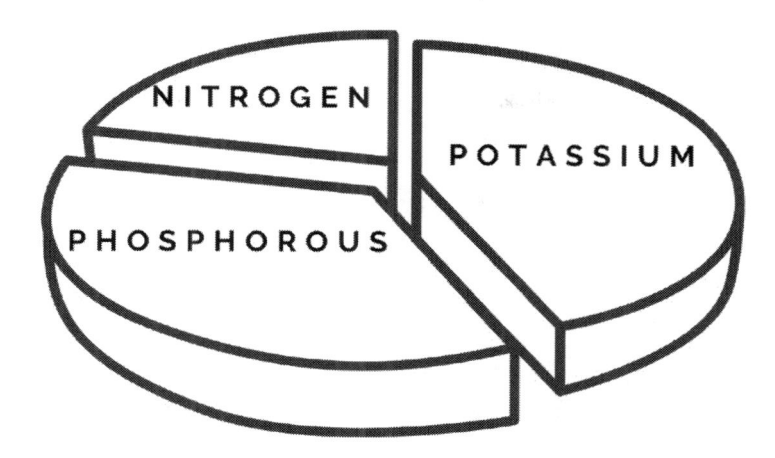

Pie chart showing Nitrogen, Potassium, and Phosphorous sections.

In the yearly chart on the next few pages, color in the month that your orchid starts sending out new roots. A) Color through the entire period, stopping when no new roots are being produced. During that phase, use more potassium.

Follow the same procedure to find out B) when the orchid produces new leaves (or pseudobulbs) and C) when it starts to send out a new flower spike. Use different colors for A, B, and C. Color them in the chart above.

Your orchid will repeat the same pattern yearly, so start implementing a change in fertilize 2 weeks before the highlighted dates.

Stages of Life	Dates	Best Fertilizer
Dormancy		---none---
Root Growth		More Potassium
Leaf Growth		More Nitrogen
In Bloom		More Phosphorous
Rebloom		More Phosphorous

YEARLY CHANGES

If you make any changes in potting media, repots, or fertilization methods, write them in the space below.

Orchid #	January	February	March	April	May	June

YEARLY FERTILIZATION

Orchid #	July	August	Sept.	Oct.	Nov.	Dec.

GENERAL NOTES

BLOOMING CYCLE

"Don't let the tall weeds cast a shadow on the beautiful flowers in your garden." – *Steve Maraboli*

This chapter will talk about how your orchid plant gets from a seed to your home, and how you can take care of it in your house. It won't focus on the stages from seed germination to the fertilization, since as an orchid hobbyist, that isn't something I'd be doing anytime soon. Just so you'll know, those parts will be mentioned, but not as the focus point of this chapter. What this chapter does mention:

> How Long do Cut Orchids Last
> How long do Blooms Last
> Do Orchids go Into Dormancy
> How Keikis (baby orchids) are produced

In the Beginning...

There are two ways that new orchids grow. The first, a keiki, is a small clone plant of the mother, carrying the same characteristics: size, color, shape, growing conditions, etc. Keiki is a Hawaiian word for baby orchid. Keikis grow on the side of the stem, developing new roots, leaves and in eight months to a year, are ready to be removed from the adult plant.

The main concern is to have patience for this keiki to grow roots before you remove it from the mother plant. Don't cut it off too soon. When there are three to four good roots, then you can remove it safely. The best place to repot the keiki is in the same pot as it's mother, since it will already be used to the lighting, watering, fertilizing and humidity in this pot.

The mother plant will also help regulate the water in the potting medium, since such a small plant by itself in a pot can easily get overwatered, breaking down the medium even more.

The second way is one I haven't yet experienced personally, but is growing from seed. This method will take quite a lot longer to produce a full blossoming orchid, anywhere from four to eight years. The seed itself will take up to two months to react and start to grow. In two years, it will produce its first leaf.

Basically, there are two ways to germinate orchids from seeds: (1) symbiotic germination, with the help of a fungus—a process named Mycorrhizae—and (2) asymbiotic germination, in petri dishes with all the necessary ingredients to germinate well.

If you have time and patience, it may be something that is worthwhile. Yet, the process is more technical than I wish to expand in this book.

As you can see, most orchid growers stick to the first method, which is hoping a keiki will grow. There are keiki pastes that you can apply to simulate growing hormones in the mother plant, if you want to step in and induce a baby orchid.

From Keiki to Adulthood

Keikis can move to their own pot once they have a strong root system and at least two well-developed leaves. From here, they are kept in extreme care, until they send out their first flower spike. Once the flower spike has appeared, they are ready to go to a greenhouse, or be placed for ordering online. In most cases, this phase can last up five years, but is mainly around three.

How are orchids pollinated?

Orchids blossom for one reason only: to attract pollinators. Outside marveling the amazing flower, the stories (or reasons) behind each flower as to why they grow that shape, or emanate a particular odor, or display certain colors is fascinating.

Each orchid has a special pollinator that it attracts. Some prefer bees, others moths and butterflies. If the animal that pollinates the orchid has nocturnal habits, then the orchid will naturally blossom at night. If the pollinator is a daytime creature, then the orchid blossoms during the day.

Some flying insects or even hummingbirds have seasonal activity, which also explains why orchids blossom in the particular season that they do. The flower is adapted to attract its preferred pollinator, often seducing it and trapping it inside the flower until the pollen sack is firmly attached to the abdomen or behind the neck. Once that task is complete, the pollinator is free to leave, going on to the next orchid.

David Horak wrote a very interesting chapter for Brooklyn Botanical Garden of several different types of orchids and how they attract pollinators. Form scent, to the flower formation, to color... One example cited in his work is the Oyphrs, which attracts a male bee. The flower is shaped like a female bee, and even produces a particular scent of a sexually active female bee. The male bee, in a flight of pure love (or lust) at first sight, lands on the labellum of the flower, and pollina is strategically attached.

The pollina which is attached to each insect (or bird) is taken to the next flower, where it comes in contact with the stigma. Once the new flower is pollinated, it will close in on itself and a seed pod will grow. Each orchid has a specific time period allow for a full seed to grow, ranging from a week to almost a full year.

...and The Orchid Life Cycle Repeats Itself

From the six steps in the life-cycle of any plant (seed, germination, growth, reproduction, pollination, and seed spreading stages) the orchid now will repeat this process for years to come.

How Long do Orchid Blooms Last?

This will depend mainly on the genus of orchid you have. Most Phalaenopsis orchids will last up to 3 months in bloom, which is why they are one of the most common orchids commercialized. Cattleyas will be open for less time, almost reaching a month in bloom.

Temperature influences orchid blooms, from halting blossoming all together all the way to stimulating orchid budding. If your orchid isn't blooming, the first reason could be not enough light, but the second (and most common one) is not a drop in the temperature at night. Phalaenopsis need a 10°F (11°C) drop in temperature at night to induce a flower spike. If this temperature is not met, it doesn't realize the seasons are changing and it keeps waiting.

According to Roger West, from the Amherst Orchid Society, once the bloom opens, you can prolong them if you do a few simple things. In his example, he uses a Cattleya orchid. It bloomed early, but he wanted to bloom a little longer for an orchid show.

Once the flowers have blossomed, he waited three or four days, then moved the plant to a cooler room. He waits this period because the flowers can take up to four days to reach their full potential. Mr. West explained that his Cattleya blooms have lasted up to eight weeks with this method.

Do Orchids go into Dormancy?

Dormancy is a period when you may think your orchid has died. After the most beautiful blossoms, they wither and fall. The "dead" orchid spike is actually alive but withers slowly. The flowers have fallen off, and the orchid doesn't grow new leaves or roots. It just sits there...immobile, lifeless, and lost. Most orchids have the sad fate of ending up in the trash during a period of dormancy.

If you're wondering, dormancy is the best time to repot, or make any changes in the orchid, since it won't react to the environment as much. The orchid has spent a lot of energy to produce the flowers and now is depleted.

Of course, that's the "newbie" explanation, because pseudobulbs store energy. The orchid needs a "vacation" from life and checks out. During this dormant period, the orchid spends less energy because it's feeding less, drinking less, photosynthesizing less... Which means you'll need to water it less and fertilize it less. It's very easy to overwater during dormancy.

Most all orchids have a recovery period from blooming, but a few genera don't, like Jewel Orchids (Lepanthes). Some of the dormancy periods are so quick that a new orchid grower might not even realize that it has come and gone.

Fun Fact: How Long do Cut Flower Spikes Last?

If you are making a floral design with orchids, a natural question is how long do the cut orchids last? Most Phalaenopsis and Oncidiums orchids will last up to 2 weeks in water, but aim for 1 week for best results. The water will have to be changed every other day. Cymbidiums and Anthuriums will last a little longer, up to 4 weeks.

How do I induce an orchid to rebloom?

The easiest way to make an orchid rebloom is cutting back the flower spike, leaving several nodes intact. This rids the spike of the old blooms, but it's still green, healthy, and sturdy enough to produce another bloom near the top. If you cut the flower spike all the way back to the base, you will induce root growth, and not a new spike.

Whether you induce a new flower spike or cut it back to induce roots, make a conscious decision. Each one will change the way you fertilize.

Please note that not all orchids have the possibility of producing a second bloom in the same season. Phalaenopsis do, but some varieties just don't. It's one blooming season, and then 6 to 8 weeks of dormancy.

How long do orchids live?

In the wild, orchids can reach up to 200 years of age, and will long survive our grandchildren. At home, the normal life-expectancy of an orchid is around 20 years.

It's very complicated to give a general answer, since there are over 28,000 genera of orchids in the world, and found in all continents except Antarctica. It also depends how well you take care of it.

Once you know how, orchids are very easy plants to cultivate. But until that knowledge is gained, your orchid could be suffering from root rot, overwatering, too much light, too little light, get watered with ice cubes, and so on. We all do this, and thankfully, we learn in time.

So, this answer to how long do orchids live is very "general", which in other words means, "wrong." In greenhouses, which do a lot better job at controlling humidity, temperature, lighting, and fertilization, they usually will do well for 40-50 years.

They may live longer than that, but each year is a little weaker than the previous. This can go on to around 50 years. In my small home office, well, I'll be good to get to 15, even with a grow light and a humidifier.

-x-x-x-x-

You've just completed the basics of orchid care and are now ready to learn the particular aspects of each genus. In the following chapters, you understand each genus in depth, so you'll have a north to guide you.

Form the specific care, you'll adapt what works within your environment and write down the specific changes to made to better adapt the orchids to where you grow them.

Tracker Tip: In the general notes for each orchid, you will have a page that looks like this →

To fill it out, write the date the orchid initiated its cycle and the day it stopped. Some cycles overlap—that's fine. It's important to fertilize the orchid according to the cycle it's in, so on the second line, write down the NPK concentration of the fertilizer you used for that cycle and how you evaluated the results.

ORCHID JOURNEY

LIFE CYCLE & FERTILIZER

Look for the key elements in fertilizer and adapt each fertilizing method to the appropriate stage. During the course of the year, cross off what you've tried. On the lines, write down what worked the best for this orchid.

K (19, Potassium, 39.098)
O (8, Oxygen, 15.999)
P (15, Phosphorus, 30.974)
B (5, Boron, 10.811)
Ca (20, Calcium, 40.078)
Mg (12, Magnesium, 24.305)

Calcium
Magnesium
Sulfur
Iron
Boron (Boric Acid)
Nirtrogen
Potassium
Cooper
Zinc
Manganese

Seaweed
Tea Bags
Epsom Salt
Banana Peel
Eggshells
Other: _____
Other: _____
Other: _____

Stages of Life
☐ Root Growth
☐ Leaf Growth
☐ Dormancy
☐ Rebloom
☐ In Bloom

Date & Best Fertilizer
_____ _____
_____ _____
_____ _____
_____ _____
_____ _____

BLOOMING CYCLE

PHALAENOPSIS

"Flowers don't worry about how they're going to bloom. They just open up and turn toward the light and that makes them beautiful."
– Jim Carrey

If your first Phalaenopsis orchid was a gift, present, or a splurge on a regular grocery store adventure, now you have a Phalaenopsis to care for.

First, congratulations!

Second, the more information you have about orchid, the better off you'll be. Soon you'll discover that caring for orchids is not as hard or complicated as you initially thought.

History, Genealogy, and Background

Let's dive into the background of Phalaenopsis (fayl-eh-NOP-sis) to understand where it came from and where it's going (as to the tropical rainforests in Southeast Asia to the best window sill in your home.)

Orchids have had a bad reputation for a long time: hard to care for, complicated, won't rebloom, die easily, expensive... But you're about to find out that this information just doesn't measure up.

Before the 1800's, they had no way of growing orchids in Europe because of the cold weather and overcast skies. Orchids thrive in bright light in tropical rainforest. Once the Wardian cases were built, which are a form of closed glass terrariums, orchids could be transported overseas and not die from the 6-week trip on a boat. This introduced orchids into the European botanical world, and from there, they spread across nations quickly.

Where were these gorgeous orchids coming from?

Phalaenopsis grow naturally in the Southeastern Asia, grasping part of Philippines, Myanmar, Thailand, China, Malaysia and Borneo. These rich lands with tropical rainforests are set in a year-round climate of 74° to 91° F (23° to 33° C). There are rains almost every day, and the humidity levels are 70 to 90 RH (Relative Humidity), remaining constant year-round.

Where did the Phalaenopsis get its complicated name?

Phalaenopsis were discovered in 1825 by Dr. C. L. Blume, a Dutch Botanist. Dr. Blume worked in Borgor (Java Island in Indonesia) as a botanist from the Royal Botanic Gardens. While on a journey through the rainforest, he saw huge white moths, almost angelic-like figures, playing around with the lush vegetation. As he approached, Dr. Blume realized these weren't moths, but Phalaenopsis orchids. The wind would play with the flower spikes, making them float effortlessly in the air.

Dr. Blume named the orchid the moth orchid, which comes from the Greek words, "Phalaina", which translates as moth, and "opsis", which is resembling, in the likeness of, appearance. The exact species he discovered was a **Phalaenopsis *ambilis***, which means charming.

Phalaenopsis in the modern-day world

Since the moth orchid made its way to Europe, thanks to the air-tight glass Wardian cases, they became accessible to the European market, yet for a precious price. These incredibly expensive plants charmed the high aristocrats. Only the wealthy could afford a Phal (or any other for that matter), and the auctions and sales were for the upper class only. Needless to say, these plants sold for tiny fortunes.

Money drives business. Orchids exploded a new form of life style: orchid hunters. The stories of these brave and courageous explorers are amazing to read, as they cross unmapped lands to find new genera and species of orchids.

Modern-Day Phalaenopsis Culture and Marketing

With the advance of technology, seeds could be germinated in labs and in petry dishes, not having to rely on manual pollination. The availability went up; the prices came down. You can purchase and adult Phal for around US$ 15-20 and a miniature Phal for around US$ 8-10.

Phals became more accessible to plant lovers and spread like a fever across the continents, becoming the number one gifted houseplant after roses.

Phalaenopsis has long outranked the Cattleya for the number one commercialized orchid. Cattleyas used to rank because of their high value in corsages and wedding bouquets. But Cattleyas stay in bloom for almost a month, maybe 5 weeks. Phalaenopsis triple that—3 months in bloom. If you're lucky, it will bloom twice.

With constant genetic adaptations and tweaks to their hybrids, Phalaenopsis can now blossom year-round (not the same plant, but different species inside the genus.) If you want a visual garden that has blooms year-round, buy one blossoming

Phalaenopsis each month. Next year, the blossoms will flower at that same time, and you'll have beautiful flowers in your indoor garden year-round.

That's all great news. But how do I care for my orchid?

What you'll have to do is recreate the natural environment that the orchid was in when they lived in the wild. Orchids are great houseplants, if you provide specific conditions that they want to live in. This means regulating the temperature, humidity, sunlight, watering, and fertilization. If you get these 5 rights, you're orchid will live for over twenty years.

Let's take each of these points one by one:

Phalaenopsis Orchid Care: Lighting

Don't place Phals in direct sunlight ever. They can't tolerate direct sunlight on their leaves. Think back to the tropical rainforest. They are lodged in the nooks of trees, hidden beneath tree branches and watered as the rain trickles down from the tree. The light is bright, since they are high up in the canopy, but leaves are still heavily shaded them from the direct rays.

They love the brightness; they hate the direct rays.

This classifies them as low-light orchids. Don't put them in the shade, because they'll die. Keep them on a window sill where they get morning sun or late evening sun. Never choose a window that has direct, hot rays during the hottest part of the day. South or east facing windows are the best, if you are in the northern hemisphere.

Before you place your orchid in a south window, look outside. Are there trees that block the sun? Is it always shaded? Is there a tall building that not only blocks your view but the light rays too? In these specific cases, another window might be better.

I have the unfortunate mishap to not get good lighting in any of my windows. So, I had to buy a grow light. Not all is lost if you also have the same conditions as mine. The good side is I can grow orchids in my home office, which I've decorated with a plant stand and a humidifier. With good taste, creativity and knowledge, you can grow your Phalaenopsis indoors with great success.

If the leaves turn a sickish-yellow color, one reason is they're getting too much sun. If the leaves are getting dark-green (which I think is particularly pretty) there isn't enough light. Move your orchids and test their locations until they are a summer toasted grass-green color.

If you have grow lights, like I do, keep them far enough away from the light that you see a faint shadow over them when you place your hand in the light's path. The shadow should not be too defined, but very fuzzy and hardly visible.

If you have a lamp that measure in foot candles (fc), then buy a set-up for 1000-1200 fc. The maximum would be 1500 fc, but that's pushing the limit. If you're using fluorescents, aim for two 4-foot 40 W fluorescent tubes a foot away from your plants.

Phalaenopsis Orchid Care: Watering

Take your Phal to the sink and open the tap water to a lukewarm temperature. Remember, these are tropical orchids. In Brazil, the rain came down like hot tea, evaporating as soon as it hit the dark asphalt. Don't use hot water by any means, but test the temperature first so it's tepid.

Take your orchid to the sink and run water over the bark, turning the pot several times, so water gets to all the areas inside the pot. Keep the water running until it flows out the bottom of the pot. Let it drain a bit, then repeat the process. You can keep the water running, but that's a lot of water that wasted.

Don't water the center (crown) of the orchid. Never do this.

Water can pool up inside the leaves and provoke bacteria, mold, fungus, and all other little microorganisms that complicate our lives as new beginner orchid growers. All these lead to one outcome: crown rot. Your orchid will start to have black spots, then a huge black splotch will take over your plant. Crown rot will kill your orchid, and it will do it quickly.

Phalaenopsis don't like to be wet all the time. Moth orchids need to have time for their roots to dry out in between watering. This isn't a general rule for all orchids.

Go back mentally to the rainforest scene. The roots absorb what they can when it rains, but soon the hot air currents move swiftly through the forest, their roots dry out. Then it rains again.

Phalaenopsis have adapted to being dry and wet, but never dry all the time or wet all the time.

In a pot, this same phenomenon of wetness and dryness is harder to achieve. That is why the potting medium is not soil, but I'll get to that in a minute. The idea is to water when the orchid is dry on the top part of the pot, but still a bit humid on the bottom. Never let a Phal totally dry up and crinkle.

Yet, if you had to pick the worse odd, overwatering kills more than occasionally forgetting to water.

There's a saying that orchids grow better when their neglected. I totally disagree, but providing too much water, too much fertilizer, too much light, too much tender, loving care—TLC, as they call it in the USA—can in fact hurt your orchid more than help it.

Phalaenopsis Orchid Care: Potting Medium

Phalaenopsis have thicker roots, which absorb the water well.

They also prefer to be humid, but dry out fast, as mentioned before. So potting medium has to be special, just for this. Commonly used potting medium for orchids are charcoal, fir bark, perlite, leca pebbles, Styrofoam, and sphagnum moss. Mix all this up together.

You can buy potting mixes already pre-made. In this case, check for a coarse-grade bark, compared to a finer grade. Fine-grade bark is used for orchids with thin, tiny roots. Phalaenopsis have thick roots, needing a thicker component to "grasp" while they're in the pot.

If you have a miniature Phalaenopsis, then you can use sphagnum moss with a finer grade bark, since the roots are more delicate and finer.

Whatever you do, don't use soil. The main objective in using a potting medium is to provide air circulation around the roots.

Phalaenopsis Orchid Care: Humidity

You've come to the final tip, and often, the most overlooked tip: find a way to raise the humidity levels in your house.

There are some orchids that thrive in near 100% relative humidity. Not Phals. They like it around 50 to 60% relative humidity.

There is an old wives' tale that says Phals will have one leaf for every percentage of humidity that they live in. I'm not sure if this is proven or not, but since they usually have 4 to 5 leaves, this seems to be true. Lower the humidity, and the leaves will crumple, wrinkle, and eventually wither away.

Beginner orchid growers also like to place their orchid in the bathroom, because that's the first humid place that comes to mind. I specifically don't recommend this because the bathroom rarely gets enough good light. Phalaenopsis like 12-14 hours of light a day during winter, and during summer, 14-16 hours

My Phalaenopsis orchid's blooms flowers have fallen off. Now what?

Your orchid is not dead, but needs some time to recuperate from the active energy that it took to produce the flower spike and blossom. Phalaenopsis orchids will enter a tiny period of dormancy—so tiny that it's hardly considered dormancy. Most Phalaenopsis actually don't have a dormancy cycle.

In any case, Phalaenopsis leaves should remain the same color and consistency, so if they are changing colors, there's something wrong.

Once the orchid produces new roots from the sides of the stem, it's time to repot and start watering and fertilizing again.

As for the flower spike, you can do two things. 1) you can cut if half way back, and encourage a new bloom, or 2) you can cut it all the way back and encourage new root growth.

If you are going for the second option, leave the spike on as long as you can (or is visually appealing) and then cut it back. The orchid reabsorbs nutrients from the spike, so they aren't wasted.

After you cut the flower spike on your moth orchid, apply cinnamon to the cut. This makes for a natural barrier that also acts as a barrier for bacteria, fungus, virus, and all those little creatures who also love orchids.

When do Phalaenopsis have to be repoted?

Every two to three years, you need to change the potting medium in your Phalaenopsis orchid.

You should repot it for the first time after the blossoms have all fallen off, so you can mark a specific date they were changed and accompany their growth from there.

Also, you don't know how the store potted your orchid. Usually, they use the worst quality ingredients since they are produced in mass.

While you are repotting, take a look at the roots to see how they are doing. Many root problems show early signs that they need repotting and you can prevent the potting mix from breaking down.

CARE SHEET
Phalaenopsis

SPECIES	FOOT CANDLES (FC)
60+	1,000-1,500

HUMIDITY
50 - 80 %

% SHADE	REPOT
70-85	2 YEARS

POTTING MIX
MEDIUM TO FINE-GRADE

FERTILIZER	WATER PREFERENCE
20-20-20	MOSTLY HUMID, BUT DRY OUT BETWEEN WATERING

DAYS BETWEEN WATERING	PH	FLOWERING
5-6	5.5-6.5	2-3 x YEAR

MAX TEMP
75-85 F
23-29 C

MIN TEMP
>60 F
>15 C

GO-TO POTTING MEDIA FOR STARTERS

65% Bark
15% sphagnum
10% Perlite
10% Charcoal — For Humid Environments

50% Bark
25% sphagnum
15% Perlite
10% Charcoal — For Arid/Dry Environments

104 - PHALAENOPSIS

ORCHID JOURNEY

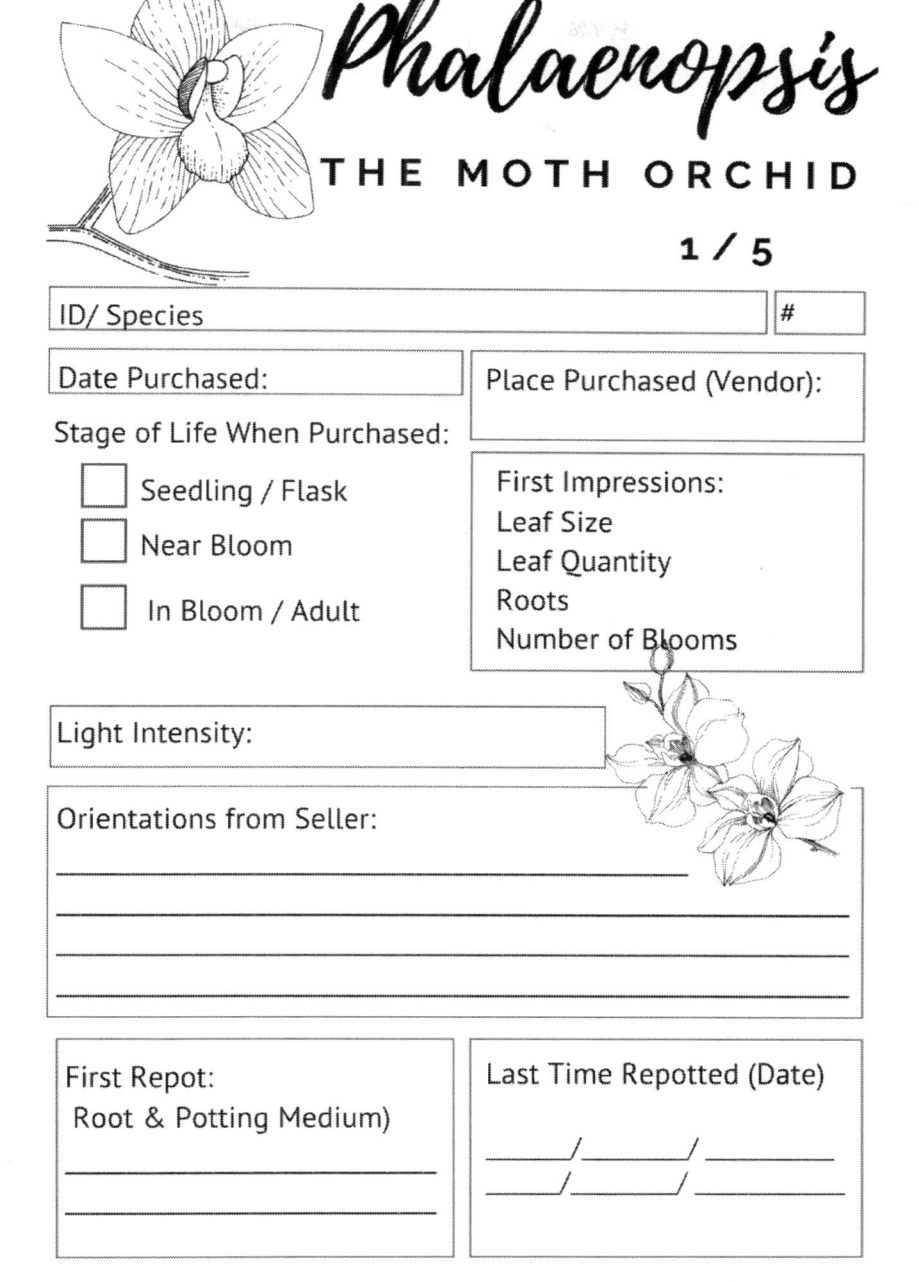

Phalaenopsis
THE MOTH ORCHID

1 / 5

| ID/ Species | # |

Date Purchased:

Place Purchased (Vendor):

Stage of Life When Purchased:

- [ ] Seedling / Flask
- [ ] Near Bloom
- [ ] In Bloom / Adult

First Impressions:
Leaf Size
Leaf Quantity
Roots
Number of Blooms

Light Intensity:

Orientations from Seller:
_____
_____
_____
_____

First Repot:
 Root & Potting Medium)
_____
_____

Last Time Repotted (Date)

____/____/____
____/____/____

PHALAENOPSIS - 105

NATURAL HABITAT

During your research, write down things like average rainfall per month, temperatures (daytime and nighttime), altitude, and any other information about this orchid's natural habitat.

ALTITUDE	AVERAGE DAYLIGHT (HOURS)

HUMIDITY

Country of Origin:
_____

JANUARY	FEBRUARY

MARCH	APRIL

MAY	JUNE	JULY	AUGUST

SEPTEMBER	OCTOBER	NOVEMBER	DECEMBER

MAX TEMP

MIN TEMP

ORCHID JOURNEY

Blooming Dates:

____/____/____
____/____/____

Dormancy Dates:

____/____/____
____/____/____

Type of Water Used
- [ ] Rain /Well Water
- [ ] Distilled
- [ ] Tap Water (pH _____)
- [ ] Other:_____

Preferred Fertilization Method

Humidity Preference

Temperature Preference

How Often to Water

Problems / Areas of Concern / Pests / Insects / Treatment:
_____
_____
_____
_____

Fragrant?
- [ ] Yes - [ ] No

Rebloomer?
- [ ] Yes - [ ] No

Likes / Dislikes
_____
_____

PHALAENOPSIS

ORCHID JOURNEY

LIFE CYCLE & FERTILIZER

Look for the key elements in fertilizer and adapt each fertilizing method to the appropriate stage. During the course of the year, cross off what you've tried. On the lines, write down what worked the best for this orchid.

Calcium
Magnesium
Sulfur
Iron
Boron (Boric Acid)
Nirtrogen
Potassium
Cooper
Zinc
Manganese

Seaweed
Tea Bags
Epsom Salt
Banana Peel
Eggshells
Other: _____
Other: _____
Other: _____

Stages of Life   **Date & Best Fertilizer**

☐ Root Growth   _____ _____

☐ Leaf Growth   _____ _____

☐ Dormancy   _____ _____

☐ Rebloom   _____ _____

☐ In Bloom   _____ _____

ORCHID JOURNEY

Awards?
☐ Yes   ☐ No

Which Awards:
_____
_____
_____
_____

What to Do Next (Action)
_____
_____

When to Do it (Time/Date)
_____
_____

Does this orchid have sentimental value? Why?
_____
_____
_____
_____

☐ Hybrid   ☐ Species

Parents (Cross):
_____
_____
_____
_____

Spike Duration

Bud Duration

Bloom Duration

Numer of Blooms

Potting Medium
☐ Sphagnum Moss
☐ Orchid Bark
☐ Hydroponics
☐ Charcoal
☐ River Rock
☐ Other: _____
☐ Other: _____

Candidate for Mounting?

PHALAENOPSIS - 109

GENERAL NOTES

ORCHID JOURNEY

Phalaenopsis

THE MOTH ORCHID

2 / 5

ID/ Species | #

Date Purchased:

Place Purchased (Vendor):

Stage of Life When Purchased:

- [ ] Seedling / Flask
- [ ] Near Bloom
- [ ] In Bloom / Adult

First Impressions:
Leaf Size
Leaf Quantity
Roots
Number of Blooms

Light Intensity:

Orientations from Seller:
_____
_____
_____
_____

First Repot:
Root & Potting Medium)
_____
_____

Last Time Repotted (Date)

____/____/____
____/____/____

PHALAENOPSIS - 111

ORCHID JOURNEY

NATURAL HABITAT

During your research, write down things like average rainfall per month, temperatures (daytime and nighttime), altitude, and any other information about this orchid's natural habitat.

ALTITUDE	AVERAGE DAYLIGHT (HOURS)

	HUMIDITY

Country of Origin: _____

JANUARY	FEBRUARY

MARCH	APRIL

MAY	JUNE	JULY	AUGUST

SEPTEMBER	OCTOBER	NOVEMBER	DECEMBER

MAX TEMP

MIN TEMP

112 - PHALAENOPSIS

ORCHID JOURNEY

Blooming Dates:

____/____/____

____/____/____

Dormancy Dates:

____/____/____

____/____/____

Type of Water Used

☐ Rain /Well Water

☐ Distilled

☐ Tap Water (pH _____)

☐ Other: _____

Preferred Fertilization Method

Humidity Preference

Temperature Preference

How Often to Water

Problems / Areas of Concern / Pests / Insects / Treatment:

_____
_____
_____
_____
_____

Fragrant?
☐ Yes ☐ No

Rebloomer?
☐ Yes ☐ No

Likes / Dislikes

_____
_____

PHALAENOPSIS - 113

ORCHID JOURNEY

LIFE CYCLE & FERTILIZER

Look for the key elements in fertilizer and adapt each fertilizing method to the appropriate stage. During the course of the year, cross off what you've tried. On the lines, write down what worked the best for this orchid.

Calcium
Magnesium
Sulfur
Iron
Boron (Boric Acid)
Nirtrogen
Potassium
Cooper
Zinc
Manganese

19 K Potassium 39.098
8 O Oxygen 15.999
15 P Phosphorus 30.974
20 Ca Calcium 40.078
5 B Boron 10.811
12 Mg Magnesium 24.305

Seaweed
Tea Bags
Epsom Salt
Banana Peel
Eggshells
Other: _____
Other: _____
Other: _____

Stages of Life   **Date & Best Fertilizer**
☐ Root Growth   _____
☐ Leaf Growth   _____
☐ Dormancy   _____
☐ Rebloom   _____
☐ In Bloom   _____

114 - PHALAENOPSIS

ORCHID JOURNEY

Awards?
☐ Yes   ☐ No

Which Awards:
_____
_____
_____
_____

What to Do Next (Action)
_____
_____

When to Do it (Time/Date)
_____
_____

Does this orchid have sentimental value? Why?
_____
_____
_____
_____

☐ Hybrid   ☐ Species

Parents (Cross):
_____
_____
_____
_____

Spike Duration

Bud Duration

Bloom Duration

Numer of Blooms

Potting Medium
☐ Sphagnum Moss
☐ Orchid Bark
☐ Hydroponics
☐ Charcoal
☐ River Rock
☐ Other: _____
☐ Other: _____

Candidate for Mounting?

PHALAENOPSIS - 115

GENERAL NOTES

ORCHID JOURNEY

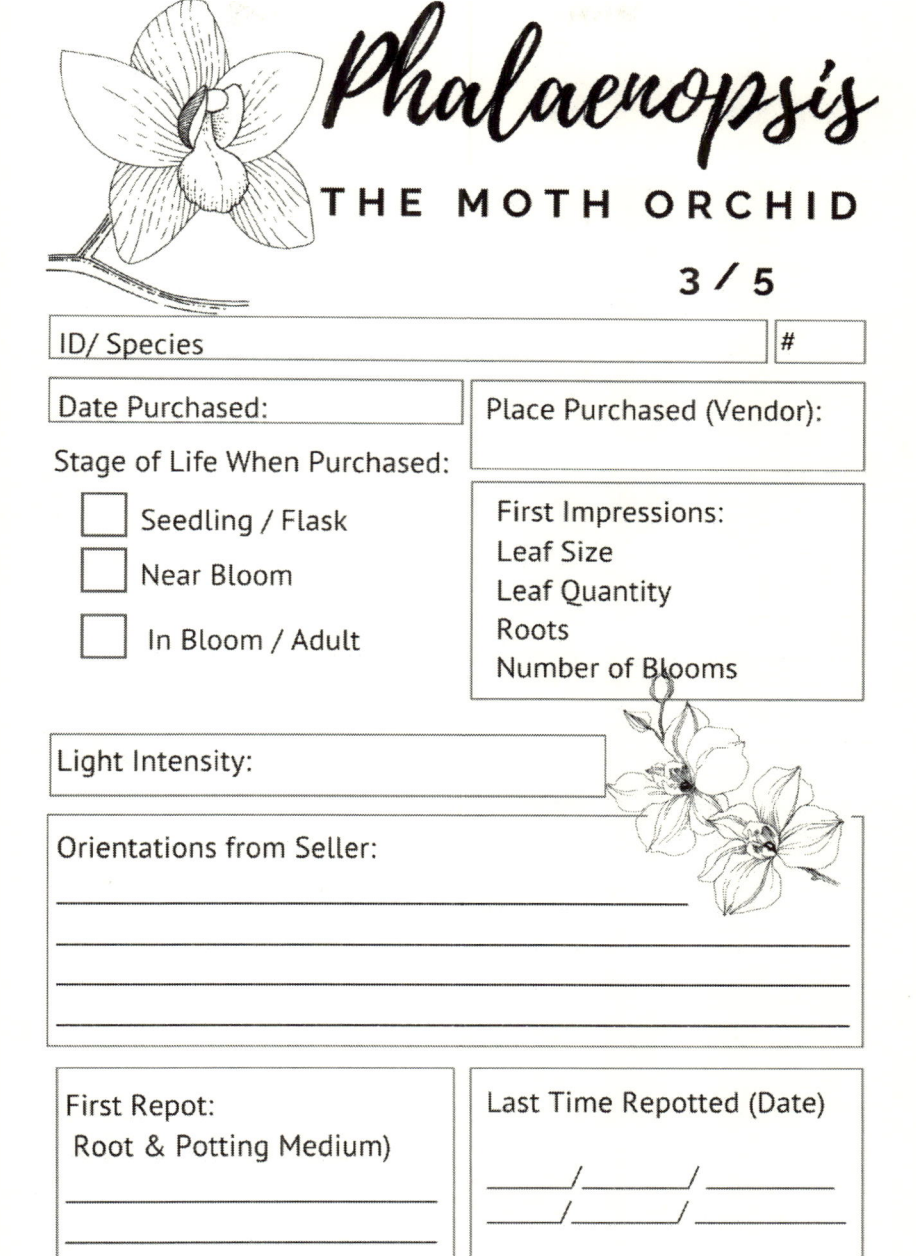

Phalaenopsis
THE MOTH ORCHID

3 / 5

ID/ Species

#

Date Purchased:

Place Purchased (Vendor):

Stage of Life When Purchased:

- [ ] Seedling / Flask
- [ ] Near Bloom
- [ ] In Bloom / Adult

First Impressions:
Leaf Size
Leaf Quantity
Roots
Number of Blooms

Light Intensity:

Orientations from Seller:
_____
_____
_____
_____

First Repot:
 Root & Potting Medium)
_____
_____

Last Time Repotted (Date)

____/____/____
____/____/____

ORCHID JOURNEY

NATURAL HABITAT

During your research, write down things like average rainfall per month, temperatures (daytime and nighttime), altitude, and any other information about this orchid's natural habitat.

ALTITUDE	AVERAGE DAYLIGHT (HOURS)

HUMIDITY

Country of Origin: _____

JANUARY	FEBRUARY
MARCH	APRIL
MAY	JUNE
JULY	AUGUST
SEPTEMBER	OCTOBER
NOVEMBER	DECEMBER

MAX TEMP

MIN TEMP

118 - PHALAENOPSIS

ORCHID JOURNEY

Blooming Dates:

____/____/____

____/____/____

Dormancy Dates:

____/____/____

____/____/____

Type of Water Used

☐ Rain /Well Water
☐ Distilled
☐ Tap Water (pH _____)
☐ Other:_____

Preferred Fertilization Method

Humidity Preference

Temperature Preference

How Often to Water

Problems / Areas of Concern / Pests / Insects / Treatment:

_____
_____
_____
_____

Fragrant?
☐ Yes ☐ No

Rebloomer?
☐ Yes ☐ No

Likes / Dislikes

_____
_____

PHALAENOPSIS - 119

ORCHID JOURNEY

LIFE CYCLE & FERTILIZER

Look for the key elements in fertilizer and adapt each fertilizing method to the appropriate stage. During the course of the year, cross off what you've tried. On the lines, write down what worked the best for this orchid.

Elements:
- Calcium
- Magnesium
- Sulfur
- Iron
- Boron (Boric Acid)
- Nirtrogen
- Potassium
- Cooper
- Zinc
- Manganese

Fertilizer sources:
- Seaweed
- Tea Bags
- Epsom Salt
- Banana Peel
- Eggshells
- Other: _____
- Other: _____
- Other: _____

Stages of Life	Date & Best Fertilizer
☐ Root Growth	_____ _____
☐ Leaf Growth	_____ _____
☐ Dormancy	_____ _____
☐ Rebloom	_____ _____
☐ In Bloom	_____ _____

120 - PHALAENOPSIS

ORCHID JOURNEY

Awards?
- [ ] Yes
- [ ] No

Which Awards:
_____
_____
_____

What to Do Next (Action)
_____
_____

When to Do it (Time/Date)
_____
_____

Does this orchid have sentimental value? Why?
_____
_____
_____

- [ ] Hybrid
- [ ] Species

Parents (Cross):
_____
_____
_____

Spike Duration
Bud Duration
Bloom Duration
Numer of Blooms

Potting Medium
- [ ] Sphagnum Moss
- [ ] Orchid Bark
- [ ] Hydroponics
- [ ] Charcoal
- [ ] River Rock
- [ ] Other: _____
- [ ] Other: _____

Candidate for Mounting?

GENERAL NOTES

ORCHID JOURNEY

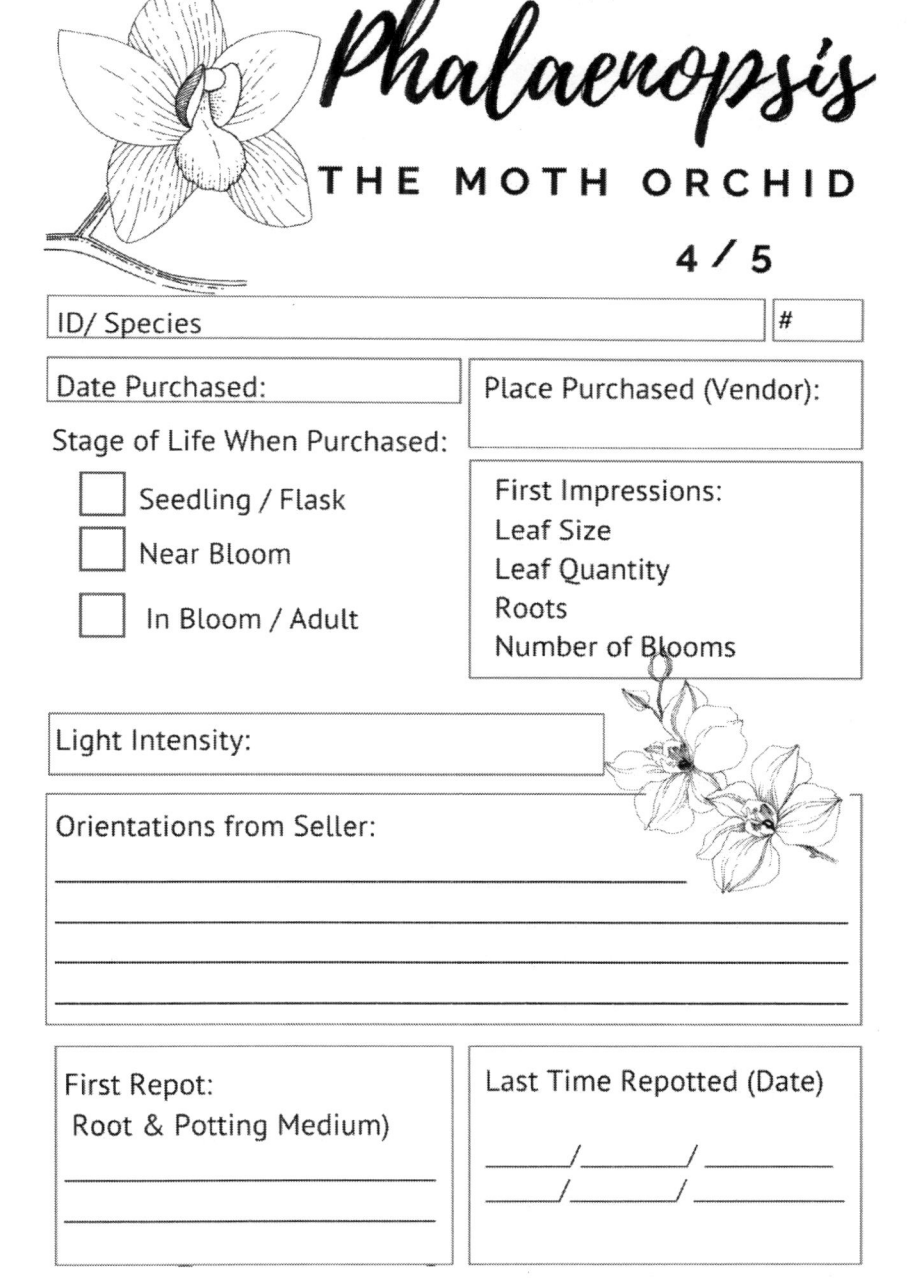

Phalaenopsis
THE MOTH ORCHID

4 / 5

| ID/ Species | # |

Date Purchased:

Place Purchased (Vendor):

Stage of Life When Purchased:

- [ ] Seedling / Flask
- [ ] Near Bloom
- [ ] In Bloom / Adult

First Impressions:
Leaf Size
Leaf Quantity
Roots
Number of Blooms

Light Intensity:

Orientations from Seller:
_____
_____
_____
_____

First Repot:
 Root & Potting Medium)
_____
_____

Last Time Repotted (Date)
___/___/_____
___/___/_____

PHALAENOPSIS - 123

ORCHID JOURNEY

NATURAL HABITAT

During your research, write down things like average rainfall per month, temperatures (daytime and nighttime), altitude, and any other information about this orchid's natural habitat.

ALTITUDE	AVERAGE DAYLIGHT (HOURS)

	HUMIDITY

Country of Origin:
_____

JANUARY	FEBRUARY

MARCH	APRIL

MAY	JUNE	JULY	AUGUST

SEPTEMBER	OCTOBER	NOVEMBER	DECEMBER

MAX TEMP

MIN TEMP

124 - PHALAENOPSIS

ORCHID JOURNEY

Blooming Dates:

____/____/____

____/____/____

Dormancy Dates:

____/____/____

____/____/____

Type of Water Used

- [ ] Rain / Well Water
- [ ] Distilled
- [ ] Tap Water (pH _____)
- [ ] Other: _____

Preferred Fertilization Method

Humidity Preference

Temperature Preference

How Often to Water

Problems / Areas of Concern / Pests / Insects / Treatment:

_____
_____
_____
_____

Fragrant?
- [ ] Yes - [ ] No

Rebloomer?
- [ ] Yes - [ ] No

Likes / Dislikes

_____
_____

PHALAENOPSIS

ORCHID JOURNEY

LIFE CYCLE & FERTILIZER

Look for the key elements in fertilizer and adapt each fertilizing method to the appropriate stage. During the course of the year, cross off what you've tried. On the lines, write down what worked the best for this orchid.

Calcium
Magnesium
Sulfur
Iron
Boron (Boric Acid)
Nirtrogen
Potassium
Cooper
Zinc
Manganese

Seaweed
Tea Bags
Epsom Salt
Banana Peel
Eggshells
Other: _____
Other: _____
Other: _____

Stages of Life

☐ Root Growth
☐ Leaf Growth
☐ Dormancy
☐ Rebloom
☐ In Bloom

Date & Best Fertilizer

_____ _____
_____ _____
_____ _____
_____ _____
_____ _____

126 - PHALAENOPSIS

ORCHID JOURNEY

Awards?
- [ ] Yes
- [ ] No

Which Awards:
_____
_____
_____
_____

What to Do Next (Action)
_____
_____

When to Do it (Time/Date)
_____
_____

Does this orchid have sentimental value? Why?
_____
_____
_____
_____

- [ ] Hybrid   - [ ] Species

Parents (Cross):
_____
_____
_____
_____

Spike Duration
Bud Duration
Bloom Duration
Numer of Blooms

Potting Medium
- [ ] Sphagnum Moss
- [ ] Orchid Bark
- [ ] Hydroponics
- [ ] Charcoal
- [ ] River Rock
- [ ] Other: _____
- [ ] Other: _____

Candidate for Mounting?

PHALAENOPSIS - 127

GENERAL NOTES

ORCHID JOURNEY

Phalaenopsis
THE MOTH ORCHID

5 / 5

ID/ Species | #

Date Purchased:

Place Purchased (Vendor):

Stage of Life When Purchased:

☐ Seedling / Flask

☐ Near Bloom

☐ In Bloom / Adult

First Impressions:
Leaf Size
Leaf Quantity
Roots
Number of Blooms

Light Intensity:

Orientations from Seller:
_____
_____
_____
_____

First Repot:
 Root & Potting Medium)
_____
_____

Last Time Repotted (Date)
____/____/____
____/____/____

ORCHID JOURNEY

NATURAL HABITAT

During your research, write down things like average rainfall per month, temperatures (daytime and nighttime), altitude, and any other information about this orchid's natural habitat.

ALTITUDE	AVERAGE DAYLIGHT (HOURS)

	HUMIDITY

Country of Origin:
_____

JANUARY	FEBRUARY

MARCH	APRIL

MAY	JUNE	JULY	AUGUST

SEPTEMBER	OCTOBER	NOVEMBER	DECEMBER

MAX TEMP

MIN TEMP

130 - PHALAENOPSIS

ORCHID JOURNEY

Blooming Dates:

____/____/____

____/____/____

Dormancy Dates:

____/____/____

____/____/____

Type of Water Used
- [ ] Rain /Well Water
- [ ] Distilled
- [ ] Tap Water (pH _____)
- [ ] Other:_____

Preferred Fertilization Method

Humidity Preference

Temperature Preference

How Often to Water

Problems / Areas of Concern / Pests / Insects / Treatment:

_____
_____
_____
_____

Fragrant?
- [ ] Yes [ ] No

Rebloomer?
- [ ] Yes [ ] No

Likes / Dislikes
_____
_____

PHALAENOPSIS - 131

ORCHID JOURNEY

LIFE CYCLE & FERTILIZER

Look for the key elements in fertilizer and adapt each fertilizing method to the appropriate stage. During the course of the year, cross off what you've tried. On the lines, write down what worked the best for this orchid.

19 K Potassium 39.098

Calcium
Magnesium
Sulfur
Iron
Boron (Boric Acid)
Nirtrogen
Potassium
Cooper
Zinc
Manganese

8 O Oxygen 15.999

Seaweed
Tea Bags
Epsom Salt
Banana Peel
Eggshells
Other: _____
Other: _____
Other: _____

15 P Phosphorus 30.974

5 B Boron 10.811

20 Ca Calcium 40.078

12 Mg Magnesium 24.305

Stages of Life

☐ Root Growth
☐ Leaf Growth
☐ Dormancy
☐ Rebloom
☐ In Bloom

Date & Best Fertilizer

_____ _____
_____ _____
_____ _____
_____ _____
_____ _____

132 - PHALAENOPSIS

ORCHID JOURNEY

Awards?
- [ ] Yes [ ] No

Which Awards:
_____
_____
_____
_____

What to Do Next (Action)
_____
_____

When to Do it (Time/Date)
_____
_____

Does this orchid have sentimental value? Why?
_____
_____
_____
_____

[ ] Hybrid [ ] Species

Parents (Cross):
_____
_____
_____
_____

Spike Duration

Bud Duration

Bloom Duration

Numer of Blooms

Potting Medium
- [ ] Sphagnum Moss
- [ ] Orchid Bark
- [ ] Hydroponics
- [ ] Charcoal
- [ ] River Rock
- [ ] Other: _____
- [ ] Other: _____

Candidate for Mounting?

ORCHID JOURNEY

GENERAL NOTES

CATTLEYA

"A flower blooming in the desert proves to the world that adversity, no matter how great, can be overcome."
– *Matshona Dhliwayo*

Cattleya orchids are common among the tropical and subtropical forests. The original Cattleya (to where the name derived) came from Pernambuco, Brazil. It can also be found in Costa Rica, Venezuela, Colombia, Peru, Guyana, and Bolivia. With the spread of information and basic Cattleya orchid care, this orchid can find its way into your living room as well, no matter where you live.

How did Cattleya orchids get their name?

Funny as it seems, it wasn't a Brazilian who named the orchid, but a British merchant in 1818. William Cattley held trading posts with several countries, the main trade being with Russia. On one of the packages that arrived from Brazil came a near-dead plant with long white tendrils.

Suspecting it was an orchid, William nurtured it back to life. Be it luck, chance, or a divine blessing, one of his cousins, John Prescott was also a horticulturist. Prescott drew many of the orchid drawings in Cattley's horticulturist books. After the beautiful orchid bloomed, they sent it to be catalogued Glasgow Botanical Gardens.

That specific orchid is now known as the Cattleya labiate.

The amazing side in this story is that two men, who knew nothing of this particular orchid's preferences, tastes, characteristics, or environment, nurtured this plant back from near death. This gives us our first clue that these orchids are not that hard to take care of and can take some beatings—a perfect specimen for new orchid growers!

Basic Care for Cattleya

To grow a Cattleya orchid, you need to observe 7 basic requirements and conditions. Even though some orchid enthusiasts will agree that Phalaenopsis orchids (moth or butterfly orchids) are the easiest for beginner orchid growers, this is the next step up. With the right information, they can be just as easy as the Phalaenopsis.

Cattleya's Light and Shade Preferences

One of the biggest reasons Cattleyas don't bloom on their yearly schedule is because of insufficient light. Cattleyas are part of the "bright light" group, by receiving their sun in the early morning or the later part of the day.

In general, Cattleyas prefer brighter light than the Phalaenopsis (moth orchids) do. If you have both, place the Cattleya closer to the light than the Phalaenopsis, who will prefer more shade.

Can Cattleya grow in full sun? No. They need a place that provides more shade than sun, actually. As for shade, Cattleyas like to be 60% of the time out of the direct sun. They still want a bright, well-lit room, but not direct beams. Don't keep your orchid in a window that gets sun at all hours—morning, noon and night. If you live in a climate that is blessed enough to grow orchids outside (lucky you), attach them to the tree that gets more shade than sun. Never attach an orchid where direct afternoon beams can scorch it.

To know if the light condition is just right, the leaves will be a pale green. If they are dark, deep green, almost a darker spinach-colored green, then the orchid isn't getting enough light. If it's receiving too much light, the leaves will turn a yellowish pale green, and black spots will occur. This could change to a darker red, almost purple color, when there hasn't been enough sun to cause the spotting, but the leaves are still feeling the heat.

Best Temperature for Cattleyas

Talking about heat, Cattleyas orchid live in the tropics and subtropics. Warm, baby, warm... If sunlight was the main cause for not obtaining new blooms each year, then the difference in temperature during day and night is the runner-up, a second-place Cattleya orchid destroyer.

In the rainforest, the daytime temperatures oscillate between 77-86° F (25-30° C) year round. This is a bit too uncomfortable to get inside a living room or office space, especially during the summer, but Cattleyas will survive at 72° F.

The problem isn't the higher range of temperatures, but the lower range. At night, Cattleyas love a drastic drop in degrees, ranging from 50-53.6° F (10-12° C). A few can endure a mid- 40° F, but none can tolerate frost.

The temperature drop will stimulate flower growth. If you have a sick Cattleya or for some other reason you don't want a flower spike, (maybe you're promoting a better root growth) then keep the temperature constant at around 70° F.

A good idea is to turn the heat off in the room with the orchid during the summer months. This can get the 15-degree temperature drop that Cattleyas are so desperately looking for. In the summer, keep the Cattleya near a slightly cracked-open window, where the cooler night air will do wonders for your orchid.

Air Movement for Cattleyas

When it comes to moving that orchid near a window, another idea would be to take the Cattleyas outside (if your weather permits.) In most of the states in the USA, this can be accomplished from late May until early October.

In addition to the temperature drop, Cattleyas will like the wind movement. I'm personally not a fan of dragging all my plants in and out each year—too much work. I just keep them inside but have a ceiling paddle fan on low all the time.

Air circulation prevents water droplets from settling on the leaves and in the orchid's crown. Dead spots occur when water doesn't evaporate, sitting on the orchid and literally drowning the orchid cells. Also, if there's a lot of water, fungal and bacterial growth occurs (both which are hard to get rid of.)

For adequate air movement, keep a low-running fan on them, night and day. The night-use of the fan is important—just as important as the day-use.

Leaves "breathe" at night.

During the day, high temperatures provoke the stomata on the leaves to close, trapping humidity inside, along with oxygen and some carbon dioxide. During gas exchange, there's always a small loss of humidity, which is natural. But if you're in a dry environment, which most living rooms are, that loss of humidity could mean life or death.

Think of how you breathe. When you exhale, water droplets leave, too, not only carbon dioxide. Same with the orchid. At night, there's less of a risk to lose humidity, since the night air is usually more humid than day-time air.

The loss of humidity is more harmful to the plant than improper gas exchange. This is why respiration occurs at night. A buoyant, cool, moist air flow will promote appropriate gas exchange without dehydrating the orchid.

Another added point to keeping a fan on at night: the leaf temperature drops, which is one of the previous goals. As mentioned before, constant air circulation during summer (or with high temperatures) can dry out low humidity rooms even more, making the room prejudicial for your Cattleya. Make sure you also have a humidifier, which brings us to the next topic: humidity.

Cattleya's Humidity Preferences

Cattleyas live in a humid environment, ranging from 40 to 70% humidity, but for a home office, aim for a humidity level from in between 40 to 55%.

The higher the humidity level, the higher the air circulation must be. Stagnant, non-moving humidity raises chances for bacterial and fungal infections. You can achieve this by:

Using humidity trays
Grouping plants together
Using a humidifier
Using a top layer of moss
Spraying or misting the room in the morning
Adding other household plants to the room

Even though common advice is to use a humidity tray, I have my doubts and concerns about the actual humidity it provides.

A humidity tray is a low pan-like tray filled with pebbles, rocks, marbles, gravel or aquarium rocks. Fill the pan half-way with water, not covering the rocks, then sit the orchid pot on top. The pot mustn't be touching water or sitting in the water.

Some orchid growers swear by this method. My practical experience says this does very little for the overall humidity. Since the evaporation in these pans dissipates into the environment around one inch above the level of water, it has no overall effect in the room's humidity levels.

If your orchid is in a small, shorter pot, practically hugging the humidity tray, it might receive some humidity, but don't expect to get a big change in humidity levels. Knowing the poor result rates, other growers advised to place several humidity trays and not only one.

I certainly don't advise investing your money in humidity trays, since you can build your own with common materials laying around your house.

Watering Cattleyas

Cattleyas will be a little different–drier—in their watering schedule than Phalaenopsis will. There is a saying that with Phals, if you think they might be thirsty, water immediately. For Cattleyas, wait another day before watering.

Determiners how fast a pot will dry are:
  Temperature – higher temperatures promote faster drying
  Air Movement – stagnant air will promote dampness, which can lead to root rot
  Light – Direct sunlight will dry out the pot faster
  Growth/Dormancy periods - during dormant periods the orchid will absorb less water
  Calendar – during winter, water less

The potting medium is the number one determiner in how long a Cattleya orchid will dry out. The more your medium is planted with sphagnum moss and charcoal, the longer humidity will remain in the pot. This is especially good for smaller, younger Cattleyas, but the older they get, the less sphagnum you'll need to use.

Cattleya Potting Mix/ Medium

Cattleyas prefer a medium grade potting mix over a finer mix. Since their roots are larger, and can handle larger objects in the mix to grip. A finer-coarse material will give them an unstable feeling, and they can topple over easily. To satisfy this condition, a good addition to your potting medium is fir bark, tree fern fiber, or larger leca pebbles (clay pebbles).

Mounted Cattleyas on cork or drift wood is one of my favorite ways to "pot" orchids. Cattleyas do well to being mounted, if you water them every day. The ventilation and freedom by not having their roots cramped inside a pot lets them feel more "at home." If you do mount a Cattleya, make sure it is getting sufficient humidity, since it will dry out faster than in a pot.

Potting and Repotting Cattleyas

As to the type of pot, many orchid enthusiasts claim that their Cattleyas prefer clay pots over plastic ones. Although this might be more of a personal preference, I don't suggest clay pots, especially if you're a new orchid grower.

Stick to the plastic pot for now, with lots of slits or abundant holes. You'll be better off. In two years when it's time to repot the Cattleya, you can definitely switch to a clay pot.

To repot the Cattleya, if it is in a clay pot, more than likely you'll need to break the pot. This is better than trying to wedge it out of the pot, ripping and damaging the roots. In a plastic pot, the Cattleya will slide out easier. Still, wiggle the plant gently, releasing the roots from the sides of the pot before yanking it out.

Choose a pot that will provide 2-3 years' worth of growth. To estimate this, mimic the space that three pseudobulbs take, add that to the plant and pick a pot that size.

Usually, Cattleyas grow 1 or 2 pseudobulbs a year. Don't overpot: choosing a pot much bigger than the orchids roots. This stresses the plant, as it looks to attach itself to the side of the pot.

When you place the Cattleya in the new pot, don't place the rhizome in the middle of the pot. This is a common mistake. Place the older rhizome near the edge of the pot, and the new growths pointing toward the center.

This encourages new roots and provides plenty of space for new growth, as it fills up, crawling toward the other side of your pot. The older rhizomes will not be harmed by placing them next to the side of the pot. They won't be growing that many roots as compared to the newer growth.

Dividing Cattleyas

How do you transplant a Cattleya orchid? If you have a bigger Cattleya and want to divide it, select three or four pseudobulbs on the rhizome and divide only after those. Any rhizome with only two pseudobulbs will not have enough energy to provide sufficient growth and will probably end up dying after being divided.

Wait until the orchid has finished blooming and all the flowers have fallen off. For most Cattleyas, this means in the spring. Once the flowers fall, the dormant cycle begins and Cattleyas will not need much energy to promote growth.

Extra tip: Extra humidity is essential right after dividing and repotting a Cattleya, so turn up the humidifier or use a top layer of sphagnum moss. Humidity is wonderful, water is not. Don't water the Cattleya for a week after repotting. If you soaked the potting mix before you used it, then this is sufficient for water supply. Also, at this stage, the risk of infection is greatly increased. Water makes it worse.

Another tip: always use sterilized utensils. You can use alcohol, a flame or any other way of sterilization. Don't trim or cut one orchid, then another one, then another… Always sterilize after cutting, trimming, dividing, etc.

One the open "wound" of the cut, apply cinnamon, the type we using in baking and sold in grocery stores. Only apply it to open cuts and never to the orchid roots. Cinnamon is a natural healer. Some growers go as far as saying that cinnamon is antibacterial, but I've had no proof of that. It does wonders, but not miracles.

Feeding/ Fertilization for Cattleyas

In comparison to Phalaenopsis, Cattleyas will need a less concentrated fertilizer. When picking a fertilizer for Cattleyas, chose one that has a lower concentration and is balanced, for example a 10-10-10 or 13-13-13. No matter which brand or NPK ratio you use, always dilute the fertilizer to ¼ of what the instructions recommend. Also, whatever fertilizer you end up choosing, make sure it is urea-free.

Too much fertilizer causes root burn and will promote salt build-up on the top of your potting medium. In Cattleyas, if you happen to over-fertilize, and the roots aren't burned, but absorbing the chemicals will promote abundant leaf and root growth, hindering the flower production.

There are reasons to temporarily hinder flower production. This might be what you're aiming for if your orchid roots are damaged and you're trying to nurture them back to life. Maybe your Cattleya got severely sunburned and you're trying to recuperate the plant, in determent to seeing a beautiful flower this season. If this is the case, use your fertilizer constantly, just avoid root burn, and only do this for a temporary period.

Tip: If your Cattleya's leaves are dark green yet still getting appropriate light, it might mean there is too much nitrogen in your fertilizer. On the other hand, if you are using a lot of fir bark, in the potting medium, you'll need to supplement. Use a fertilizer with a higher nitrogen count, like 30-10-10, since fir bark retains more nitrogen from the atmosphere than other material, like clay pebbles.

Fertilization in Dormant Seasons

There are two types of Cattleyas when it comes to fertilization: those who bloom year-round, and those that go dormant. If your Cattleya has a dormant cycle, blooming only once a year, then you'll need to cut back on water and fertilization during this dormant cycle (usually this coincides with winter, but observe your plant to make sure.) The dormancy cycle could be only a few weeks, too.

Some Cattleyas go dormant up to a few months. Don't think in terms of six months, but a shorter period. If your Cattleya blooms all the time, keep up the light, fertilizer, and watering to a normal schedule, never cutting down. To observe when the Cattleya leaves the dormancy cycle, you'll see new roots starting to shoot out from the stem.

What time of year do Cattleya bloom?

Most cattleyas produce only one flower blossom period a year, usually toward the end of summer or late winter. For floral design, this is extremely useful to know, because you can plant two together, a summer bloomer and a winter bloomer. Your orchid design will have flowers most the year round, and not just leaves. While one is in bloom, the other is getting ready to produce buds.

Flowers in Cattleya are extremely fragrant and exotic. Note: some Cattleyas don't have a scent, but when they do...wow.

Cattleyas are what usually comes mind when thinking of orchids, with the moth orchid (Phalaenopsis) in second place. For the longest time, they were the number one selling orchid in the USA, but due to how much longer the moth orchid keeps their flowers (up to 4 months) they have lost that ranking.

How long do Cattleya blooms last?

One to three weeks is the general answer for most Cattleyas. Even though Cattleyas are slow growers—five to seven years from seed to a mature adult—their flowers are well worth the wait.

ORCHID JOURNEY

CARE SHEET

Cattleya

SPECIES	FOOT CANDLES (FC)
45+	3,000 - 5,000

HUMIDITY
40-70%

% FULL SUN	REPOT
50-70	2-3 YEARS

POTTING MIX
MEDIUM-GRADE

FERTILIZER	WATER PREFERENCE
30-10-10	MOSTLY DRY, BUT THIRSTY DRINKERS, PREFERING LOTS OF WATER

DAYS BETWEEN WATERING	PH	FLOWERING
7-10	5.0 - 7.0	1-2 x YEAR

MAX TEMP
70-90 F / 21-32 C

MIN TEMP
55-60 F / 12-15 C

GO-TO POTTING MEDIA FOR STARTERS

SOILESS MATERIAL, SUCH AS RIVER ROCKS, PEBBLES, CHARCOAL, PUMICE, OR PEA PEBBLES.

IF YOUR AREA IS DRY, ADD SPHAGNUM MOSS

ORCHID JOURNEY

Cattleya

THE CORSAGE ORCHID

1 / 5

| ID/ Species | # |

Date Purchased:

Place Purchased (Vendor):

Stage of Life When Purchased:
- [ ] Seedling / Flask
- [ ] Near Bloom
- [ ] In Bloom / Adult

First Impressions:
Leaf Size
Leaf Quantity
Roots
Number of Blooms

Light Intensity:

Orientations from Seller:
_____
_____
_____

First Repot:
(Root & Potting Medium)
_____
_____

Last Time Repotted (Date)

_____ / _____ / _____

_____ / _____ / _____

CATTLEYA - 147

ORCHID JOURNEY

NATURAL HABITAT

During your research, write down things like average rainfall per month, temperatures (daytime and nighttime), altitude, and any other information about this orchid's natural habitat.

ALTITUDE	AVERAGE DAYLIGHT (HOURS)

	HUMIDITY

Country of Origin: _____

JANUARY	FEBRUARY

MARCH	APRIL

MAY	JUNE	JULY	AUGUST

SEPTEMBER	OCTOBER	NOVEMBER	DECEMBER

MAX TEMP

MIN TEMP

148 - CATTLEYA

ORCHID JOURNEY

Blooming Dates:

____/____/____

____/____/____

Dormancy Dates:

____/____/____

____/____/____

Type of Water Used

☐ Rain /Well Water

☐ Distilled

☐ Tap Water (pH _____)

☐ Other:_____

Preferred Fertilization Method

Humidity Preference

Temperature Preference

How Often to Water

Problems / Areas of Concern / Pests / Insects / Treatment:

_____
_____
_____
_____

Fragrant?

☐ Yes ☐ No

Rebloomer?

☐ Yes ☐ No

Likes / Dislikes

_____
_____

CATTLEYA - 149

ORCHID JOURNEY

LIFE CYCLE & FERTILIZER

Look for the key elements in fertilizer and adapt each fertilizing method to the appropriate stage. During the course of the year, cross off what you've tried. On the lines, write down what worked the best for this orchid.

Calcium
Magnesium
Sulfur
Iron
Boron (Boric Acid)
Nirtrogen
Potassium
Cooper
Zinc
Manganese

Seaweed
Tea Bags
Epsom Salt
Banana Peel
Eggshells
Other: _____
Other: _____
Other: _____

Stages of Life

- [ ] Root Growth
- [ ] Leaf Growth
- [ ] Dormancy
- [ ] Rebloom
- [ ] In Bloom

Date & Best Fertilizer

_____ _____
_____ _____
_____ _____
_____ _____
_____ _____

150 - CATTLEYA

ORCHID JOURNEY

Awards?
- [ ] Yes   [ ] No

Which Awards:
_____
_____
_____
_____

What to Do Next (Action)
_____
_____

When to Do it (Time/Date)
_____
_____

Does this orchid have sentimental value? Why?
_____
_____
_____
_____

[ ] Hybrid   [ ] Species

Parents (Cross):
_____
_____
_____
_____

Spike Duration

Bud Duration

Bloom Duration

Numer of Blooms

Potting Medium
- [ ] Sphagnum Moss
- [ ] Orchid Bark
- [ ] Hydroponics
- [ ] Charcoal
- [ ] River Rock
- [ ] Other: _____
- [ ] Other: _____

Candidate for Mounting?

CATTLEYA - 151

ORCHID JOURNEY

GENERAL NOTES

152 - CATTLEYA

ORCHID JOURNEY

Cattleya
THE CORSAGE ORCHID

2 / 5

| ID/ Species | # |

Date Purchased:

Place Purchased (Vendor):

Stage of Life When Purchased:
- [ ] Seedling / Flask
- [ ] Near Bloom
- [ ] In Bloom / Adult

First Impressions:
Leaf Size
Leaf Quantity
Roots
Number of Blooms

Light Intensity:

Orientations from Seller:
_____
_____
_____

First Repot:
(Root & Potting Medium)
_____
_____

Last Time Repotted (Date)
____/____/_____
____/____/_____

CATTLEYA - 153

ORCHID JOURNEY

NATURAL HABITAT

During your research, write down things like average rainfall per month, temperatures (daytime and nighttime), altitude, and any other information about this orchid's natural habitat.

ALTITUDE	AVERAGE DAYLIGHT (HOURS)

	HUMIDITY

Country of Origin:
_____

JANUARY	FEBRUARY
MARCH	APRIL
MAY	JUNE	JULY	AUGUST
SEPTEMBER	OCTOBER	NOVEMBER	DECEMBER

MAX TEMP

MIN TEMP

- CATTLEYA

ORCHID JOURNEY

Blooming Dates:

_____/_____/_____

_____/_____/_____

Dormancy Dates:

_____/_____/_____

_____/_____/_____

Type of Water Used

☐ Rain /Well Water
☐ Distilled
☐ Tap Water (pH _____)
☐ Other:_____

Preferred Fertilization Method

Humidity Preference

Temperature Preference

How Often to Water

Problems / Areas of Concern / Pests / Insects / Treatment:

_____
_____
_____
_____

Fragrant? ☐ Yes ☐ No

Rebloomer? ☐ Yes ☐ No

Likes / Dislikes

_____
_____

CATTLEYA - 155

ORCHID JOURNEY

LIFE CYCLE & FERTILIZER

Look for the key elements in fertilizer and adapt each fertilizing method to the appropriate stage. During the course of the year, cross off what you've tried. On the lines, write down what worked the best for this orchid.

Calcium
Magnesium
Sulfur
Iron
Boron (Boric Acid)
Nirtrogen
Potassium
Cooper
Zinc
Manganese

Seaweed
Tea Bags
Epsom Salt
Banana Peel
Eggshells
Other: _____
Other: _____
Other: _____

Stages of Life

- [ ] Root Growth
- [ ] Leaf Growth
- [ ] Dormancy
- [ ] Rebloom
- [ ] In Bloom

Date & Best Fertilizer

_____ _____

_____ _____

_____ _____

_____ _____

_____ _____

156 - CATTLEYA

ORCHID JOURNEY

Awards?
- [ ] Yes
- [ ] No

Which Awards:
_____
_____
_____

What to Do Next (Action)
_____
_____

When to Do it (Time/Date)
_____
_____

Does this orchid have sentimental value? Why?
_____
_____
_____
_____

- [ ] Hybrid
- [ ] Species

Parents (Cross):
_____
_____
_____

Spike Duration

Bud Duration

Bloom Duration

Numer of Blooms

Potting Medium
- [ ] Sphagnum Moss
- [ ] Orchid Bark
- [ ] Hydroponics
- [ ] Charcoal
- [ ] River Rock
- [ ] Other: _____
- [ ] Other: _____

Candidate for Mounting?

CATTLEYA - 157

GENERAL NOTES

ORCHID JOURNEY

Cattleya 3/5
THE CORSAGE ORCHID

| ID/ Species | # |

Date Purchased:

Place Purchased (Vendor):

Stage of Life When Purchased:

☐ Seedling / Flask

☐ Near Bloom

☐ In Bloom / Adult

First Impressions:
Leaf Size
Leaf Quantity
Roots
Number of Blooms

Light Intensity:

Orientations from Seller:
_____
_____
_____

First Repot:
(Root & Potting Medium)
_____
_____

Last Time Repotted (Date)

_____/_____/_____

_____/_____/_____

ORCHID JOURNEY

NATURAL HABITAT

During your research, write down things like average rainfall per month, temperatures (daytime and nighttime), altitude, and any other information about this orchid's natural habitat.

ALTITUDE	AVERAGE DAYLIGHT (HOURS)

HUMIDITY

Country of Origin:
_____

JANUARY	FEBRUARY
MARCH	APRIL
MAY	JUNE	JULY	AUGUST
SEPTEMBER	OCTOBER	NOVEMBER	DECEMBER

MAX TEMP

MIN TEMP

_____
_____
_____
_____
_____

160 - CATTLEYA

ORCHID JOURNEY

Blooming Dates:

____/____/____
____/____/____

Dormancy Dates:

____/____/____
____/____/____

Type of Water Used

- [ ] Rain /Well Water
- [ ] Distilled
- [ ] Tap Water (pH _____)
- [ ] Other:_____

Preferred Fertilization Method

Humidity Preference

Temperature Preference

How Often to Water

Problems / Areas of Concern / Pests / Insects / Treatment:
_____
_____
_____
_____

Fragrant? [ ] Yes [ ] No

Rebloomer? [ ] Yes [ ] No

Likes / Dislikes
_____
_____

CATTLEYA

ORCHID JOURNEY

LIFE CYCLE & FERTILIZER

Look for the key elements in fertilizer and adapt each fertilizing method to the appropriate stage. During the course of the year, cross off what you've tried. On the lines, write down what worked the best for this orchid.

Calcium
Magnesium
Sulfur
Iron
Boron (Boric Acid)
Nirtrogen
Potassium
Cooper
Zinc
Manganese

Seaweed
Tea Bags
Epsom Salt
Banana Peel
Eggshells
Other: _____
Other: _____
Other: _____

Stages of Life

☐ Root Growth
☐ Leaf Growth
☐ Dormancy
☐ Rebloom
☐ In Bloom

Date & Best Fertilizer

_____ _____
_____ _____
_____ _____
_____ _____
_____ _____

162 - CATTLEYA

ORCHID JOURNEY

Awards?
- [ ] Yes
- [ ] No

Which Awards:
_____
_____
_____
_____

What to Do Next (Action)
_____
_____

When to Do it (Time/Date)
_____
_____

Does this orchid have sentimental value? Why?
_____
_____
_____
_____

- [ ] Hybrid
- [ ] Species

Parents (Cross):
_____
_____
_____

Spike Duration

Bud Duration

Bloom Duration

Numer of Blooms

Potting Medium
- [ ] Sphagnum Moss
- [ ] Orchid Bark
- [ ] Hydroponics
- [ ] Charcoal
- [ ] River Rock
- [ ] Other: _____
- [ ] Other: _____

Candidate for Mounting?

CATTLEYA - 163

ORCHID JOURNEY

GENERAL NOTES

ORCHID JOURNEY

Cattleya
THE CORSAGE ORCHID

4 / 5

| ID/ Species | # |

Date Purchased:

Place Purchased (Vendor):

Stage of Life When Purchased:
- [ ] Seedling / Flask
- [ ] Near Bloom
- [ ] In Bloom / Adult

First Impressions:
Leaf Size
Leaf Quantity
Roots
Number of Blooms

Light Intensity:

Orientations from Seller:
_____
_____
_____

First Repot:
(Root & Potting Medium)
_____
_____

Last Time Repotted (Date)

_____/_____/_____

_____/_____/_____

CATTLEYA - 165

ORCHID JOURNEY

NATURAL HABITAT

During your research, write down things like average rainfall per month, temperatures (daytime and nighttime), altitude, and any other information about this orchid's natural habitat.

ALTITUDE	AVERAGE DAYLIGHT (HOURS)
	HUMIDITY

Country of Origin: _____

JANUARY	FEBRUARY
MARCH	APRIL
MAY	JUNE	JULY	AUGUST
SEPTEMBER	OCTOBER	NOVEMBER	DECEMBER

MAX TEMP _____
_____
_____

MIN TEMP _____
_____
_____

166 - CATTLEYA

ORCHID JOURNEY

Blooming Dates:

____/____/____

____/____/____

Dormancy Dates:

____/____/____

____/____/____

Type of Water Used

☐ Rain /Well Water
☐ Distilled
☐ Tap Water (pH _____)
☐ Other: _____

Preferred Fertilization Method

Humidity Preference

Temperature Preference

How Often to Water

Problems / Areas of Concern / Pests / Insects / Treatment:

_____
_____
_____
_____

Fragrant? ☐ Yes ☐ No

Rebloomer? ☐ Yes ☐ No

Likes / Dislikes

_____
_____

CATTLEYA - 167

ORCHID JOURNEY

LIFE CYCLE & FERTILIZER

Look for the key elements in fertilizer and adapt each fertilizing method to the appropriate stage. During the course of the year, cross off what you've tried. On the lines, write down what worked the best for this orchid.

Calcium
Magnesium
Sulfur
Iron
Boron (Boric Acid)
Nirtrogen
Potassium
Cooper
Zinc
Manganese

Seaweed
Tea Bags
Epsom Salt
Banana Peel
Eggshells
Other: _____
Other: _____
Other: _____

Stages of Life

☐ Root Growth
☐ Leaf Growth
☐ Dormancy
☐ Rebloom
☐ In Bloom

Date & Best Fertilizer

_____ _____
_____ _____
_____ _____
_____ _____
_____ _____

168 - CATTLEYA

ORCHID JOURNEY

Awards?
☐ Yes   ☐ No

Which Awards:
_____
_____
_____
_____

What to Do Next (Action)
_____
_____

When to Do it (Time/Date)
_____
_____

Does this orchid have sentimental value? Why?
_____
_____
_____
_____

☐ Hybrid   ☐ Species

Parents (Cross):
_____
_____
_____

Spike Duration
Bud Duration
Bloom Duration
Numer of Blooms

Potting Medium
☐ Sphagnum Moss
☐ Orchid Bark
☐ Hydroponics
☐ Charcoal
☐ River Rock
☐ Other: _____
☐ Other: _____

Candidate for Mounting?

CATTLEYA - 169

GENERAL NOTES

ORCHID JOURNEY

Cattleya

THE CORSAGE ORCHID

5 / 5

| ID/ Species | # |

Date Purchased:

Place Purchased (Vendor):

Stage of Life When Purchased:
- [ ] Seedling / Flask
- [ ] Near Bloom
- [ ] In Bloom / Adult

First Impressions:
Leaf Size
Leaf Quantity
Roots
Number of Blooms

Light Intensity:

Orientations from Seller:
_____
_____
_____

First Repot:
(Root & Potting Medium)
_____
_____

Last Time Repotted (Date)

____/____/____

____/____/____

ORCHID JOURNEY

NATURAL HABITAT

During your research, write down things like average rainfall per month, temperatures (daytime and nighttime), altitude, and any other information about this orchid's natural habitat.

ALTITUDE	AVERAGE DAYLIGHT (HOURS)

	HUMIDITY

Country of Origin: _____

JANUARY	FEBRUARY
MARCH	APRIL
MAY	JUNE	JULY	AUGUST
SEPTEMBER	OCTOBER	NOVEMBER	DECEMBER

MAX TEMP

MIN TEMP

ORCHID JOURNEY

Blooming Dates:

____/____/____

____/____/____

Dormancy Dates:

____/____/____

____/____/____

Type of Water Used

☐ Rain /Well Water
☐ Distilled
☐ Tap Water (pH _____)
☐ Other:_____

Preferred Fertilization Method

Humidity Preference

Temperature Preference

How Often to Water

Problems / Areas of Concern / Pests / Insects / Treatment:

_____
_____
_____
_____
_____

Fragrant?
☐ Yes ☐ No

Rebloomer?
☐ Yes ☐ No

Likes / Dislikes

_____
_____

CATTLEYA - 173

ORCHID JOURNEY

LIFE CYCLE & FERTILIZER

Look for the key elements in fertilizer and adapt each fertilizing method to the appropriate stage. During the course of the year, cross off what you've tried. On the lines, write down what worked the best for this orchid.

K 19 Potassium 39.098

Calcium
Magnesium
Sulfur
Iron
Boron (Boric Acid)
Nirtrogen
Potassium
Cooper
Zinc
Manganese

O 8 Oxygen 15.999

Seaweed
Tea Bags
Epsom Salt
Banana Peel
Eggshells
Other: _____
Other: _____
Other: _____

P 15 Phosphorus 30.974

B 5 Boron 10.811

Ca 20 Calcium 40.078

Mg 12 Magnesium 24.305

Stages of Life

☐ Root Growth
☐ Leaf Growth
☐ Dormancy
☐ Rebloom
☐ In Bloom

Date & Best Fertilizer

_____ _____
_____ _____
_____ _____
_____ _____
_____ _____

174 - CATTLEYA

ORCHID JOURNEY

Awards?
☐ Yes   ☐ No

Which Awards:
_____
_____
_____

What to Do Next (Action)
_____
_____

When to Do it (Time/Date)
_____
_____

Does this orchid have sentimental value? Why?
_____
_____
_____
_____

☐ Hybrid   ☐ Species

Parents (Cross):
_____
_____
_____

Spike Duration

Bud Duration

Bloom Duration

Numer of Blooms

Potting Medium
☐ Sphagnum Moss
☐ Orchid Bark
☐ Hydroponics
☐ Charcoal
☐ River Rock
☐ Other: _____
☐ Other: _____

Candidate for Mounting?

CATTLEYA

GENERAL NOTES

DENDROBIUM

"Even the tiniest of flowers can have the toughest roots."
– *Shannon Mullen*

When we think about the types of Dendrobiums, we usually divided them into two groups or categories, the soft cane Dendrobiums and the hard cane Dendrobiums. Even though that is correct and those two groups exist technically, they are not the correct way to classify Dendrobiums.

Others might think that the two classifications are Nobile and Phalaenopsis since those are the most widely known orchids. Again, this isn't even close. Cultivation, care, and culture will differ, and Dendrobiums have been classified into more ways than just two distinct groupings.

The Dendrobium genus is the 2nd largest orchid genus with over 1,400 cataloged species, only losing to Bulbophyllum, which comes in at 1st place. These orchids grow in a vast array of conditions: from monsoons near tropical rainforest, to cool and drier climates near mountains.

They have so many differences between the species that it's almost impossible to write a general care and culture guide for them. Besides the fact that they are light-loving orchids, there is one thing it you can guarantee for having good growth on your Dendrobium orchid—ensuring good roots.

What are the different types of Dendrobium orchids that exist?

The Dendrobium genus is classified into 5 distinct groups: Dendrobium phalaenopsis, Dendrobium spatulata, Dendrobium latouria, Dendrobium formosae, and simply Dendrobium. Each has their one growing requirements, culture, care, and specific patterns of growth. This group of 5 isn't the only way to classify them.

Habitat and Cultivation of the Dendrobium Orchids

The name Dendrobium offers little to suffice that gap since it comes from Greek and literally means "life on a tree". Sadly, this describes all epiphytic orchids. Since the Dendrobium genus is so vast, the growing conditions and culture vary from day to night, which is why it is important to know what type of Dendrobium you have so you can grow it well.

Dendrobium orchids are some of the most diverse orchids that exist, growing in vast areas that all differ in climate, altitude, humidity, and lighting. They grow from sea level up to 12,000 ft (3660 m).

When you hear things like, "Dendrobiums are hard to grow," or the famous, "I can't grow a Dendrobium. They just don't like me," don't fall into this line of thinking. Maybe the species they had was not the correct one for their climate and routine, or maybe they choose a species that was hard for beginners. In the Dendrobium genus, there are orchids from beginners to advance-growing orchids.

Before the Pangea, orchids grew natively in what is now Asia. With the spreading of the continents, you can now find Dendrobiums all around China, Japan, Malaysia, Philippines,

India, and in Australia. The majority of the species come from Papa New Guinea, where over 500 species have been cataloged. Don't take Papa New Guinea's hot and humid weather and lowland altitude as an all-inclusive guideline. Since Dendrobiums have scattered over such a large area is so huge, some have adapted to live in monsoon climates and others in extremely dry, cooler climates.

The one unifying element that ties this group together is the fact that they like to be rootbound in tiny pots and all like to receive bright light. All Dendrobiums have shorter roots (compared to the length of their canes) and need to have the pot fitting tightly around them. Everything else varies.

If you are new to Dendrobiums (and all other orchids as well), it's best to start out with a hybrid and not a "pure" species. As the name suggests, a hybrid is a mix of two parent species. Since species are very acclimated to their environment, if you make mistakes with watering, lighting, or fertilizing, they won't be as forgiving as a hybrid will. A hybrid will have a mixture of the two parents, so they can cover more ground with mistakes. A hybrid will also more accustomed to living in wider conditions, with more options for cultivation.

Some are deciduous, which means the leaves fall off during winter as the orchid will take a short rest, called dormancy. The orchid will appear dead.

The other classification (besides deciduous) is called persistent, which means they will take no winter rest (or a tiny winter rest), but the leaves still might fall. This is contrasted to evergreen, where the leaves never drop.

In the rest of this chapter, you'll learn the five main divisions of the Dendrobium genus. Each one has specific care and growth patterns, as mentioned above.

1) Dendrobium Phalaenanthe

These Dendrobiums resemble the moth-shaped flower of the Phalaenopsis orchid, and that similarity is why they received this name. Den-phals, as they are also called, are warm growers, preferring higher light than the others. This category is classified as good beginner orchids since they are fairly easy to maintain healthy during the year. They are also the most commonly found to purchase since they are the most hybridized on the market.

The pseudobulbs on these orchids are not fat nor rounded but similar to cylindrical canes that grow quite large, 2 to 4 feet (0.6 m to 1.2 m). It's uncommon to hear them being referred to as pseudobulbs since they are called mostly "canes". Their smaller rubbery leaves are around 3 to 6 inches (7.6 to 15 cm) long.

On a new plant, the orchid will produce up to 5 inflorescences at a time. An older plant will reward you with around 20 inflorescences, beautifully hanging around the small pot.

Since these are warm-growers, found mainly in northeastern Australia and in areas near the equator, don't drop the winter temperature lower than 50° F (10° C) and don't push the upper limit above 90° F (32.2° C). The warm weather usually implies more watering, but whatever you do, let them dry out before watering again. When you water, use tons of water, more so than other orchids of its kind. Put it this way: they're thirsty and drink tons but like to rest well before drinking again.

They don't like the moist environment all the time, which makes them similar to the watering cycle of a Cattleya but unlike the Phalaenopsis.

They will also need a rest from water, breaking the cycle twice a year. You should not water them during these short periods. Still, they are considered persistent (and do not have a dormancy cycle), but they aren't deciduous. In another very respected classification of Horticultural Groups of Dendrobiums elaborated by Rebecca Tyson Northern, these orchids would be classified as Type VI.

Some Examples of Species:
Dendrobium affine
Dendrobium bigibbum
Dendrobium lithicolum
Dendrobium phalaenopsis
Dendrobium superbiens

Note: Phalaenopsis and Bigibbum were once considered to be the same species. They are now separated, but you still might encounter a few "misnamed" orchids using the former classification.

2)   **Dendrobium Spatulata**

Spatulata orchids have long, horn-like projections that spiral into unique-shaped flowers, similar to an antelope horns or insect antennas. They are sometimes classified as Antelope Dendrobiums because of this. There are somewhere near 50 species of Dendrobium Spatulatas, all science-fiction or alien-looking with intricate detail in each blossom—absolutely fascinating!

Dendrobium Spatulata orchids are hot, tropical orchids and unlike the first category, they don't require a rest period. These orchids bloom several times a year. That is why they are classified as persistent and not deciduous. The culture and care of Dendrobium Spatulata are somewhat similar to the Phalaenanthe orchids, but without the rest period, longer light periods, and tons more of water.

They also like intermediate temperatures all year long, with no winter drop in degrees.

As for light, they are intermediate to high light orchids, but instead of placing them in a similar group to Cattleyas and

Vandas, just prolong the time they are exposed to filtered light. They will do well outside and can get full sunlight as long as it is not during the hottest part of the day.

In another classification, this group is known as Type V, but can also overlap, containing hybrids of type VI, too.

The sad part is that these orchids (Dendrobium spatulata) are not recommended for beginners since they prefer higher humidity and higher light requirements that mimic tropical climates, which are hard to keep constant all year round.

Some Examples of Species:

Dendrobium antennatum	Dendrobium lasianthera
Dendrobium canaliculatum	Dendrobium lineale
Dendrobium carronii	Dendrobium stratiotes
Dendrobium cochliodes	Dendrobium strebloceras
Dendrobium discolor	Dendrobium sutiknoi
Dendrobium gouldii	Dendrobium tangerinum
Dendrobium Helix	Dendrobium williamsianum

Some Examples of Hybrids:
Dendrobium Christabella
Dendrobium Lorrie Mortimer
Dendrobium Linc's Jewel
Dendrobium Retrorocket
Dendrobium Touch of Gold

3) Dendrobium

Dendrobiums are probably the most common type of Dendrobium species due to the famous Dendrobium Nobile. Most people think of this purple flower with the white center when they visualize a Dendrobium. They can have two types of

Dendrobiums, the pendulous or the erect. In the pendulous group, the flowers cascade from the base and flow over the pot, as the Nobile does. In the erect, they grow upward, and as time goes by, the weight of the flower increases from the flower spike in bloom, they slowly form a slight curve.

Nobile orchids are found in cooler-growing climates, or higher altitudes. They thrive in the cooler mountain bases of Southeast Asia, mostly southern China. including Dendrobiums are also found in neighboring countries such as Burma, Thailand, Nepal, parts of India, and Vietnam.

Even though these countries get quite hot, they also have mountainous regions, where the Dendrobiums can be found. In these cooler temperatures of around 80 F (27 C) during the day and at night drop to mid-sixties, 66 F (20C). Research says that Dendrobiums can tolerate a few days of close to freezing temperatures. Even though it's cool, the humidity stays high: 60 to 80% humidity (which is absolutely perfect for root rot. Be careful).

They need a full winter's rest of watering, and this is apparent as the leaves fall off. In another classification, Dendrobiums are referred to as the type I.

Some Examples of Species:

Dendrobium anosmum
Dendrobium chrysanthum
Dendrobium crepidatum
Dendrobium devonianum
Dendrobium falconeri
Dendrobium fimbriatum
Dendrobium findlayanum
Dendrobium moniliforme
Dendrobium moniliforme
Dendrobium moschatum
Dendrobium nobile
Dendrobium primulinum
Dendrobium signatum
Dendrobium stuarti

4)   Dendrobium Latouria

There are around 60 orchid species of Dendrobium Latouria, most of which inhabit the land around New Guinea, Philippines, and Samoa. Some of these orchids have hairy labellums (lips, or the bottom petal where the pollinator can land). The Dendrobium Latouria orchids are short and stumpy-looking, with smaller rhizomes and pseudobulbs (compared to the cane-like Pseudobulbs).

Dendrobium Latouria orchids are not only epiphytes, but some can be. A few of these Dendrobiums can be terrestrial, growing in subalpine grasslands. These orchids are extremely good for intermediate beginners since they can tolerate mild mistakes and are more lenient as we learn and adapt our care for them.

The only thing they don't forgive is not enough light. They are high light orchids. Living near the equator yet in a higher altitude, they hardly have a winter adjustment at all. Keep the orchid in light and with plenty of water, and a little drier in winter, during its rest.

Some Examples of Species:
Dendrobium aberrans
Dendrobium alexanderae
Dendrobium atroviolaceum
Dendrobium bifalce
Dendrobium convolutum
Dendrobium engae
Dendrobium eximium

Dendrobium finisterrae
Dendrobium forbesii
Dendrobium johnsoniae
Dendrobium macrophyllum
Dendrobium polysema
Dendrobium rhodostictum
Dendrobium spectabile

Some Examples of Hybrids:
Dendrobium Roy Tokunaga
Dendrobium Stephen Batchelor

Dendrobium Andree Millar
Dendrobium Bill Takamatsu
Dendrobium Wonder Nishii

5) Dendrobium Formosae

These orchids grow quite large so make space for cultivating them. Their blossoms, which can get up to four inches (10.6 cm) are spectacular when in bloom, hence the name Formosa.

The Portuguese sailors and mariners named the island of Taiwan "Formosa" in 1522 since Formosa means beautifully formed, majestically made. In Brazil, this term is used to describe a beautifully-graceful woman.

Another name for this orchid group is the Nigrohirsutae type.

There are originally from the cooler regions in Southeast Asia, in countries such as Vietnam, Laos, India, China, and Burma. This means that Dendrobium Formosae enjoy the monsoon weather, with heavy rains and high sun, followed by a cooler season where they dry out. To recreate this same effect, you can suspend watering in early autumn.

Some Examples of Species:

Dendrobium bellatulum
Dendrobium cruentum
Dendrobium dearie
Dendrobium draconis
Dendrobium formosum
Dendrobium infundibulum
Dendrobium sanderae
Dendrobium scabrilingue
Dendrobium schuetzei
Dendrobium sinense
Dendrobium tobaense
Dendrobium trigon

There is always more than one way to do things, which made this chapter especially hard to write. While researching, I found 3 different ways to classify Dendrobiums. I wish things fell into nice, neatly-compacted categories, but as it turns out, life just isn't like that.

There other categories of Dendrobium orchids not mentioned above, which depending on who you read, are placed in different spots. Some overlap... It all depends on who you read and who is writing.

Several orchids may fit into separate categories such as Callista (or Densiflora), Dendrocoryone (which are found in Australia), Calcarifera, Calyptrochilus, Dockrillia, and the Pedilonum orchids

To know how to better care for your Dendrobium orchid, research the name of your orchid to find out more about your orchid's specific growing conditions. Look for items such as temperature, humidity, lighting, altitude, and fertilization. Try to mimic the same growing conditions of your Dendrobium orchid and you're half the way there.

Dendrobium Roots

One thing is that is common to all Dendrobiums is that to have a healthy one, you need to have healthy roots. Even if the canes are nice, thick, and healthy, if the roots aren't, then you're Dendrobium will suffer.

To have healthy Dendrobium roots, you must guarantee 5 conditions are met:

(1) the Dendrobium orchid needs to be rootbound,
(2) potted in a high-drainage medium,
(3) be free of pests and insects,
(4) receive sufficient water, and
(5) have all dead roots removed.

1)   The Dendrobium roots need to be rootbound

Dendrobiums have shorter roots for the elongated size of their canes. The top growth is quite heavy and long, and we tend to look at the tiny pot and wonder how they ever grow. Reacting in tender loving care towards what we think is a suffering orchid, we repot it into a pot that is vastly larger than it needs.

Dendrobium's roots need to be rootbound and underpotted for several reasons. If they don't adhere to the sides of the pot, the long canes will not have the stability they need. This can cause the pot to topple over. If you want, you can add rocks to the bottom of the pot for additional weight. Terracotta pots are excellent choices for dendrobiums because they provide both the stability, cooler temperatures, and higher humidity that some Dendrobium species require.

Always stake your Dendrobium orchid, especially after a repot. The orchid's roots aren't deep or strong enough to support the weight or height of the canes. Staking guarantees your orchid won't be shaking around in the pot, destroying or damaging new roots.

Rhizome clips are another way to keep the Dendrobium orchid secure in the pot until it becomes root bound. Since the new roots are not that deep, a rhizome clip—a metal wire that fastens onto the side of the pot and crosses the diameter of the top media—holds the rhizome down into the media and prevents it from lifting or moving when new growth starts.

2) Roots need to have a High-Drainage Medium

Dendrobium roots (for the most part) like to be heavily watered. Out of the 1,400 species of orchids that englobe the Dendrobium genus, most are water-thirsty orchids. If their medium doesn't drain properly, they will not breathe inside the pot. Contrary to popular belief, the overwatering doesn't cause root rot, but the lack of circulating air inside the media.

In a pot, they don't have that privilege. If they didn't like as much water as they do—Dendrobiums are similar to Cattleyas in there watering preferences in that they like to dry out before being soaked again—then having a media that absorbed water would be preferred. But since they constantly like to be watered, and constantly like to dry out afterward, they need to have the appropriate medium.

Stay away from coconut husks and fibers. In the past, they have been used for Dendrobiums, but recently (as in the last 10-15 years) the salt content in them is way too high for the orchid roots to tolerate. The high salt burns them over time. They also hold more moisture than the Dendrobium would like, and the roots become damaged with the excessive water.

Most orchid growers have had success with leca beads (didn't work for me) and orchid bark (bark worked). Again, find a medium that you feel comfortable with and learn from it.

3) Dendrobium Roots need to be Free of Pests

Since Dendrobiums require higher water levels, they can also attract insects that prefer higher humidity. Inside the potting medium is a perfect place for little critters to hide out and create an infestation. The most common pests include scale, aphids, thrips, false spider mites, and snails.

In any case, the life of a Dendrobium orchid is in its roots. If it doesn't have healthy roots, it won't show any signs of life. You can add more water, increase sunlight, add fertilizer supplements, but if the root system isn't good, your Dendrobium will not gain from your effort.

Contrary to the bugs that inhabit the sphagnum moss, most Dendrobium pests and insects do not live in the potting medium. They rather make their way around the canes, where they suck the sap out of the leaf and pseudobulb. They bore into the roots and shoots, feeding on the orchid juices and sap.

4) Dendrobium Roots must Receive Plenty of Water

Most of the 1,400 species of Dendrobium orchids need more water during active growth. Some are dormant, where you'll need to suspend or diminish the water quantity and quality for a few months

Dendrobiums (for the most part) will like to receive more water than a Phalaenopsis does, wanting to partially dry out before another watering. Don't ever let the media get too dry, though. Keep the bottom 1/3 moist at all times—moist, not soggy.

The first sign of not watering enough is that the Dendrobium canes will shrivel and look extremely wrinkled. What is happening is that the roots are not absorbing the water you are providing, or you are not providing enough water—both will cause dehydration.

If the Dendrobium canes aren't wrinkled but have small wedges or creases, you're doing fine with your watering schedule.

If you are watering too much or too often (overwatering is in 2 aspects: quantity and frequency) the first sign that is visible is root rot. If this rot continues, it will travel upward to the canes and cause pseudobulb rot.

5) Remove all Dead Dendrobium Roots

When it comes time to repot, after the first new Dendrobium roots shoot out but haven't reached the potting medium yet, it's time to repot. There is nothing worse for your orchid than to have dead roots inside a space that already is disputed.

All dead roots have to go. If they stay inside the pot, they decompose due to the bacteria that is already present. Yet this chemical release signals to other bacteria that this potting media is a vast source of energy and nutrients, and they spread like wildfire. Fungus, which feeds on bacteria, also infects the scenario. Months later, your orchid has hardly any live roots left.

Decomposing roots are natural since roots aren't meant to live forever. That is why each new season, your Dendrobium orchid sends out new roots and leaves. These die off naturally, except in nature, they fall to the ground. They don't stay in close contact with the orchid, as the rootbound and underpotted Dendrobium roots are.

Be extra careful to remove all dead, mushy, non-resilient roots. Press on the roots to verify their firmness. Color is not always the best indication since roots that do not receive light will be naturally yellow. Squeeze and note their firmness. If they squish between your fingers, cut them off. Any Dendrobium roots that are brittle even after watering also need to be cut off.

Dendrobium Shriveled Canes

Shriveled canes on a Dendrobium can cause certain discomfort. Why are they there? Should I cut them? Will they induce more flowers if cut? Are they a sign of dehydration? When your Dendrobium orchid shows signs of shriveled canes, you have several options. The most important is to know what caused the pseudobulb to wrinkle and proceed from there.

Dendrobium canes will shrivel due to the end of a normal life cycle, after blossoming has occurred, lack of water or nutrients, and an infection of some kind. These wrinkled canes are to be expected in most of the cases, but you have to be sure which one.

Causes for Shriveled Dendrobium Canes	
End of the orchid's life cycle	No Action Required Cut Canes if Dead
Right after Blooming	No Action required Leave Canes on Plant
Lack of Water	Water Twice Weekly Check Roots and Repot
Infection or Pests	Check for Insects

Normal Indications of Dendrobium Shriveled Canes

Dendrobium orchids undergo a year's cycle of rest (called dormancy), producing new roots, sprouting new leaves, and finally producing buds. It's a good idea to keep a calendar on the first year of orchid growing so you'll know what to expect each month/season for that particular orchid. For example, not all Dendrobiums have a rest period—den-phals don't.

Independent of having a strict dormant cycle, every year your Dendrobium will repeat the same cycle for its species. Even if the orchid has undergone some serious and stressful situations, the cycle maintains. In that case, it might not bloom but root and leaf growth should still be on par.

In this normal annual cycle, the flowers shall wilt then die. It's part of life. After the flowers drop, the canes will start to shrink in diameter and slightly wrinkle, caving into themselves. They have used their energy to produce beautiful blossoms and their nutrient supply is low. The grooves in the cane should NOT be very deep, nor visibly pronounced. If they are, then your orchid is dehydrated.

This is the time when they enter a winter's rest period. In any case, you have nothing to worry about. Just let your orchid do its thing.

Dead Dendrobium Canes

In the next year's cycle, the old Dendrobium canes can still produce buds and blossom. They shouldn't be cut off or disposed of. Even when they don't bloom, they still provide nutrients, water, and energy to keep the new growth alive.

After a few years, all the energy has been depleted of the old cane and now there is nothing left but dry, paper-like stalks. These eye-sore pseudobulbs do nothing for the orchid except provide possible entrances for bugs, pests, and insects.

These dead, shriveled Dendrobium canes should be cut off.

If you are in doubt of whether the cane is dead, cut the furthest part of the cane. If the middle is yellowish-brown, it's dead. Keep cutting closer to the rhizome until speckles of green start to appear—stop! You've cut too far. There shouldn't be green anywhere in the dead pseudobulb/cane.

Indications of Dehydration in Shriveled Dendrobiums

If your Dendrobium cane is shrinking and shriveled and the flower is about to bloom, in bloom, or any other time except rest, then this may be a sign that it's not getting enough water and is dehydrated. The wrinkles or grooves will de deeper than a normal dormancy cycle and they don't plump back up ever.

Your orchid will also display other signs that it is dehydrated. The leaves will slightly wilt, turning leathery and cracked. The leaves also droop, as if they were going through depression with no cause to live for. They just dangle, with no resilience of resistance to being folded.

Increase both watering duration and frequency for a week. The deep groves shall not disappear or push back out to plumpness, but you'll be saving your orchid from lack of water. Once a Dendrobium orchid has withered canes, it won't ever go back to completely normal. The withered effects are permanent. The expectation is to plump out slightly, yet the deep grooves will remain.

Supplying extra water is advised only if you know that your orchid has a decent root system. There is no point in watering if your Dendrobium has no healthy roots to soak up the water. If the leaves appear to have perked up after that first week of watering, then you're good. If not, unpot the orchid and take a look at the roots. The shriveled Dendrobium cane may be a cause of insufficient roots that just don't provide the water they need from the start.

Infections that Cause Dendrobium Canes to Shrivel

The last reason a Dendrobium cane shrivels is due to outside influence. This can be in form of bacteria, fungus, pests, or insects. A bacterial infection that isn't treated properly can kill the cane in all of 2 weeks. Root rot, when not cared for, will also have the same affect.

Some insect burrow through the plant tissue and even though you don't see visible signs on the exterior of the cane, they are inside feasting on a highly nutritional buffet. The otherwise healthy orchid starts to wilt. This is visible when only one of the canes withers, usually the youngest cane since the plant tissue is softer, while all the rest are plump.

Should you cut the shriveled Dendrobium canes?

After a few years, there might be a quite substantive amount of old, paper-like canes hanging off your orchid. These darker canes with a yellowish-brown color should only be removed if you guarantee for a fact, they are dead. If there is any chance that they are still alive, why remove them? After all, they are supplying nutrients to the new growth.

Does cutting canes promote more flowers?

Cutting canes from spent Dendrobiums is not ideal. This idea appeared first with phalaenopsis orchids, where cutting the flower spike after blossoming would induce more flowers. Yet these are two separate genera and anatomical structures; what applies to one can hinder the other.

For starters, a flower spike is not the same thing as a cane. When you cut off a cane, you are essentially destroying the nutrient storage of the orchid. Its life storage unit has just been removed. For a flower spike, it will grow back naturally, inducing more blossoms; a Dendrobium cane will not.

In second place, if you cut off a shriveled Dendrobium cane thinking that will induce more flowers, you just cut off the place where the flowers would be induced. Phalaenopsis orchids don't produce flower spikes from pseudobulbs because they don't have pseudobulbs. They sprout from the stem of the orchid, thus are safe to cut off. Dendrobium Phalaenopsis orchids will imitate this same pattern of growth, but other Dendrobiums grow closer to the cane. Make sure you double-check what you are about to cut.

Older canes can still produce buds and flowers, so don't cut them thinking this will induce more growth. It won't.

Propagation through old canes

Older, wrinkled Dendrobium canes may be used to propagate new orchids. Some growers who cut old canes and with proper hydration and care, say this cane shall use its energy to produce a keiki on the side. Once the keikis has a decent root system, it can be potted. This method only works if there are sufficient nutrients in the old cane.

CARE SHEET

Dendrobium

(NOBILE)

SPECIES	FOOT CANDLES (FC)
1,500+	3,000-4,000

HUMIDITY
60% (WINTER) - 80% (SUMMER)

% BRIGHT SHADE	REPOT
30-50	2 YEARS

POTTING MIX
MEDIUM-GRADE

FERTILIZER	WATER PREFERENCE
20-10-20	MOIST WHEN IN GROWTH PERIOD, BUT DRY OUT DURING DORMANCY

DAYS BETWEEN WATERING	PH	FLOWERING
1X A WEEK SUMMER, LESS DURING WINTER	5.5-6.5	1x YEAR

MAX TEMP
65-80 F
18-27 C

MIN TEMP
40-50 F
4-10 C

GO-TO POTTING MEDIA FOR STARTERS

50% Bark
25% sphagnum
15% Perlite
10% Charcoal

ORCHID JOURNEY

Dendrobiums
THE 2ND LARGEST ORCHID GENUS

1 / 5

| ID/ Species | # |

Date Purchased:

Place Purchased (Vendor):

Stage of Life When Purchased:
- [ ] Seedling / Flask
- [ ] Near Bloom
- [ ] In Bloom / Adult

First Impressions:
Leaf Size
Leaf Quantity
Roots
Number of Blooms

Light Intentsity:

Orientations from Seller:
_____
_____
_____

First Repot:
(Root & Potting Medium)
_____
_____

Last Time Repotted (Date)
____/____/____

DENDROBIUM - 197

ORCHID JOURNEY

NATURAL HABITAT

During your research, write down things like average rainfall per month, temperatures (daytime and nighttime), altitude, and any other information about this orchid's natural habitat.

ALTITUDE		AVERAGE DAYLIGHT (HOURS)

HUMIDITY

JANUARY	FEBRUARY

MARCH	APRIL

Country of Origin:
_____

MAY	JUNE	JULY	AUGUST

SEPTEMBER	OCTOBER	NOVEMBER	DECEMBER

MAX TEMP

MIN TEMP

198 - DENDROBIUM

ORCHID JOURNEY

Blooming Dates:

____/____/____

____/____/____

Dormancy Dates:

____/____/____

____/____/____

Type of Water Used

☐ Rain /Well Water
☐ Distilled
☐ Tap Water (pH _____)
☐ Other: _____

Preferred Fertilization Method

Humidity Preference

Temperature Preference

How Often to Water

Problems / Areas of Concern / Pests / Insects / Treatment:

_____
_____
_____
_____

Fragrant?
☐ Yes ☐ No

Rebloomer?
☐ Yes ☐ No

Likes / Dislikes
_____
_____

DENDROBIUM - 199

ORCHID JOURNEY

LIFE CYCLE & FERTILIZER

Look for the key elements in fertilizer and adapt each fertilizing method to the appropriate stage. During the course of the year, cross off what you've tried. On the lines, write down what worked the best for this orchid.

Calcium
Magnesium
Sulfur
Iron
Boron (Boric Acid)
Nirtrogen
Potassium
Cooper
Zinc
Manganese

Seaweed
Tea Bags
Epsom Salt
Banana Peel
Eggshells
Other: _____
Other: _____
Other: _____

Stages of Life

☐ Root Growth
☐ Leaf Growth
☐ Dormancy
☐ Rebloom
☐ In Bloom

Date & Best Fertilizer

_____ _____
_____ _____
_____ _____
_____ _____
_____ _____

200 - DENDROBIUM

ORCHID JOURNEY

Awards?
- [ ] Yes - [ ] No

Which Awards:
_____
_____
_____

What to Do Next (Action)
_____
_____

When to Do it (Time/Date)
_____
_____

Does this orchid have sentimental value? Why?
_____
_____
_____

- [ ] Hybrid - [ ] Species

Parents (Cross):
_____
_____
_____

Spike Duration

Bud Duration

Bloom Duration

Numer of Blooms

Potting Medium
- [ ] Sphagnum Moss
- [ ] Orchid Bark
- [ ] Hydroponics
- [ ] Charcoal
- [ ] River Rock
- [ ] Other: _____
- [ ] Other: _____

Candidate for Mounting?

DENDROBIUM

GENERAL NOTES

Dendrobiums

THE 2ND LARGEST ORCHID GENUS

2 / 5

| ID/ Species | # |

Date Purchased:

Place Purchased (Vendor):

Stage of Life When Purchased:
- [ ] Seedling / Flask
- [ ] Near Bloom
- [ ] In Bloom / Adult

First Impressions:
Leaf Size
Leaf Quantity
Roots
Number of Blooms

Light Intentsity:

Orientations from Seller:
_____
_____
_____

First Repot:
(Root & Potting Medium)
_____
_____
_____

Last Time Repotted (Date)

____/____/____
____/____/____

ORCHID JOURNEY

NATURAL HABITAT

During your research, write down things like average rainfall per month, temperatures (daytime and nighttime), altitude, and any other information about this orchid's natural habitat.

ALTITUDE	AVERAGE DAYLIGHT (HOURS)

HUMIDITY

Country of Origin: _____

JANUARY	FEBRUARY
MARCH	APRIL
MAY	JUNE	JULY	AUGUST
SEPTEMBER	OCTOBER	NOVEMBER	DECEMBER

MAX TEMP

MIN TEMP

204 - DENDROBIUM

ORCHID JOURNEY

Blooming Dates:

____/____/____
____/____/____

Dormancy Dates:

____/____/____
____/____/____

Type of Water Used

☐ Rain /Well Water
☐ Distilled
☐ Tap Water (pH _____)
☐ Other:_____

Preferred Fertilization Method

Humidity Preference

Temperature Preference

How Often to Water

Problems / Areas of Concern / Pests / Insects / Treatment:

_____
_____
_____
_____

Fragrant?
☐ Yes ☐ No

Rebloomer?
☐ Yes ☐ No

Likes / Dislikes
_____
_____

DENDROBIUM

ORCHID JOURNEY

LIFE CYCLE & FERTILIZER

Look for the key elements in fertilizer and adapt each fertilizing method to the appropriate stage. During the course of the year, cross off what you've tried. On the lines, write down what worked the best for this orchid.

19 K Potassium 39.098

Calcium
Magnesium
Sulfur
Iron
Boron (Boric Acid)
Nirtrogen
Potassium
Cooper
Zinc
Manganese

8 O Oxygen 15.999

Seaweed
Tea Bags
Epsom Salt
Banana Peel
Eggshells
Other: _____
Other: _____
Other: _____

15 P Phosphorus 30.974

20 Ca Calcium 40.078

5 B Boron 10.811

12 Mg Magnesium 24.305

Stages of Life

☐ Root Growth
☐ Leaf Growth
☐ Dormancy
☐ Rebloom
☐ In Bloom

Date & Best Fertilizer

_____ _____
_____ _____
_____ _____
_____ _____
_____ _____

206 - DENDROBIUM

ORCHID JOURNEY

Awards?
- [ ] Yes
- [ ] No

Which Awards:
_____
_____
_____
_____

What to Do Next (Action)
_____
_____

When to Do it (Time/Date)
_____
_____

Does this orchid have sentimental value? Why?
_____
_____
_____
_____

- [ ] Hybrid
- [ ] Species

Parents (Cross):
_____
_____
_____
_____

| Spike Duration |
| Bud Duration |
| Bloom Duration |
| Numer of Blooms |

Potting Medium
- [ ] Sphagnum Moss
- [ ] Orchid Bark
- [ ] Hydroponics
- [ ] Charcoal
- [ ] River Rock
- [ ] Other: _____
- [ ] Other: _____

Candidate for Mounting?

GENERAL NOTES

Dendrobiums

THE 2ND LARGEST ORCHID GENUS

3 / 5

| ID/ Species | # |

Date Purchased:

Place Purchased (Vendor):

Stage of Life When Purchased:
- [ ] Seedling / Flask
- [ ] Near Bloom
- [ ] In Bloom / Adult

First Impressions:
Leaf Size
Leaf Quantity
Roots
Number of Blooms

Light Intentsity:

Orientations from Seller:
_____
_____
_____

First Repot:
(Root & Potting Medium)
_____
_____
_____

Last Time Repotted (Date)

___/___/___
___/___/___

ORCHID JOURNEY

NATURAL HABITAT

During your research, write down things like average rainfall per month, temperatures (daytime and nighttime), altitude, and any other information about this orchid's natural habitat.

ALTITUDE	AVERAGE DAYLIGHT (HOURS)

HUMIDITY

Country of Origin: _____

JANUARY	FEBRUARY
MARCH	APRIL
MAY	JUNE	JULY	AUGUST
SEPTEMBER	OCTOBER	NOVEMBER	DECEMBER

MAX TEMP

MIN TEMP

ORCHID JOURNEY

Blooming Dates:

____/____/____

____/____/____

Dormancy Dates:

____/____/____

____/____/____

Type of Water Used

- [ ] Rain /Well Water
- [ ] Distilled
- [ ] Tap Water (pH _____)
- [ ] Other: _____

Preferred Fertilization Method

Humidity Preference

Temperature Preference

How Often to Water

Problems / Areas of Concern / Pests / Insects / Treatment:

_____
_____
_____
_____

Fragrant?
- [ ] Yes - [ ] No

Rebloomer?
- [ ] Yes - [ ] No

Likes / Dislikes

_____
_____

DENDROBIUM - 211

ORCHID JOURNEY

LIFE CYCLE & FERTILIZER

Look for the key elements in fertilizer and adapt each fertilizing method to the appropriate stage. During the course of the year, cross off what you've tried. On the lines, write down what worked the best for this orchid.

K 19 Potassium 39.098

Calcium
Magnesium
Sulfur
Iron
Boron (Boric Acid)
Nirtrogen
Potassium
Cooper
Zinc
Manganese

O 8 Oxygen 15.999

Seaweed
Tea Bags
Epsom Salt
Banana Peel
Eggshells
Other: _____
Other: _____
Other: _____

P 15 Phosphorus 30.974

Ca 20 Calcium 40.078

B 5 Boron 10.811

Mg 12 Magnesium 24.305

Stages of Life

☐ Root Growth
☐ Leaf Growth
☐ Dormancy
☐ Rebloom
☐ In Bloom

Date & Best Fertilizer

_____ _____
_____ _____
_____ _____
_____ _____
_____ _____

- DENDROBIUM

ORCHID JOURNEY

Awards?
- [ ] Yes
- [ ] No

Which Awards:
_____
_____
_____
_____

What to Do Next (Action)
_____
_____

When to Do it (Time/Date)
_____
_____

Does this orchid have sentimental value? Why?
_____
_____
_____
_____

- [ ] Hybrid
- [ ] Species

Parents (Cross):
_____
_____
_____
_____

Spike Duration

Bud Duration

Bloom Duration

Numer of Blooms

Potting Medium
- [ ] Sphagnum Moss
- [ ] Orchid Bark
- [ ] Hydroponics
- [ ] Charcoal
- [ ] River Rock
- [ ] Other: _____
- [ ] Other: _____

Candidate for Mounting?

DENDROBIUM - 213

GENERAL NOTES

Dendrobiums

THE 2ND LARGEST ORCHID GENUS

4 / 5

| ID/ Species | # |

Date Purchased:

Place Purchased (Vendor):

Stage of Life When Purchased:
- [ ] Seedling / Flask
- [ ] Near Bloom
- [ ] In Bloom / Adult

First Impressions:
Leaf Size
Leaf Quantity
Roots
Number of Blooms

Light Intentsity:

Orientations from Seller:
_____
_____
_____

First Repot:
(Root & Potting Medium)
_____
_____
_____

Last Time Repotted (Date)

____/____/_____
____/____/_____

ORCHID JOURNEY

NATURAL HABITAT

During your research, write down things like average rainfall per month, temperatures (daytime and nighttime), altitude, and any other information about this orchid's natural habitat.

ALTITUDE	AVERAGE DAYLIGHT (HOURS)

HUMIDITY

Country of Origin: _____

JANUARY	FEBRUARY
MARCH	APRIL
MAY	JUNE	JULY	AUGUST
SEPTEMBER	OCTOBER	NOVEMBER	DECEMBER

MAX TEMP	
	_____

MIN TEMP	
	_____

216 - DENDROBIUM

ORCHID JOURNEY

Blooming Dates:

____/____/____

____/____/____

Dormancy Dates:

____/____/____

____/____/____

Type of Water Used

☐ Rain /Well Water
☐ Distilled
☐ Tap Water (pH _____)
☐ Other:_____

Preferred Fertilization Method

Humidity Preference

Temperature Preference

How Often to Water

Problems / Areas of Concern / Pests / Insects / Treatment:

_____
_____
_____
_____

Fragrant?
☐ Yes ☐ No

Rebloomer?
☐ Yes ☐ No

Likes / Dislikes

_____
_____

DENDROBIUM - 217

ORCHID JOURNEY

LIFE CYCLE & FERTILIZER

Look for the key elements in fertilizer and adapt each fertilizing method to the appropriate stage. During the course of the year, cross off what you've tried. On the lines, write down what worked the best for this orchid.

19 K Potassium 39.098

Calcium
Magnesium
Sulfur
Iron
Boron (Boric Acid)
Nirtrogen
Potassium
Cooper
Zinc
Manganese

8 O Oxygen 15.999

Seaweed
Tea Bags
Epsom Salt
Banana Peel
Eggshells
Other: _____
Other: _____
Other: _____

15 P Phosphorus 30.974

20 Ca Calcium 40.078

5 B Boron 10.811

12 Mg Magnesium 24.305

Stages of Life

☐ Root Growth
☐ Leaf Growth
☐ Dormancy
☐ Rebloom
☐ In Bloom

Date & Best Fertilizer

_____ _____
_____ _____
_____ _____
_____ _____
_____ _____

218 - DENDROBIUM

ORCHID JOURNEY

Awards?
- [ ] Yes   - [ ] No

Which Awards:
_____
_____
_____
_____

What to Do Next (Action)
_____
_____

When to Do it (Time/Date)
_____
_____

Does this orchid have sentimental value? Why?
_____
_____
_____
_____

- [ ] Hybrid   - [ ] Species

Parents (Cross):
_____
_____
_____
_____

| Spike Duration |
| Bud Duration |
| Bloom Duration |
| Numer of Blooms |

Potting Medium
- [ ] Sphagnum Moss
- [ ] Orchid Bark
- [ ] Hydroponics
- [ ] Charcoal
- [ ] River Rock
- [ ] Other: _____
- [ ] Other: _____

Candidate for Mounting?

DENDROBIUM - 219

GENERAL NOTES

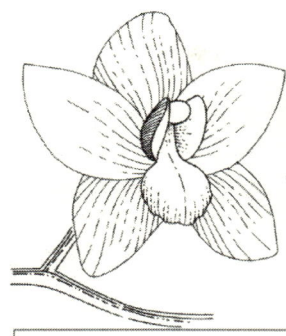

Dendrobiums

THE 2ND LARGEST ORCHID GENUS

5 / 5

| ID/ Species | # |

Date Purchased:

Place Purchased (Vendor):

Stage of Life When Purchased:

- [ ] Seedling / Flask
- [ ] Near Bloom
- [ ] In Bloom / Adult

First Impressions:
Leaf Size
Leaf Quantity
Roots
Number of Blooms

Light Intentsity:

Orientations from Seller:
_____
_____
_____

First Repot:
(Root & Potting Medium)
_____
_____

Last Time Repotted (Date)

____/____/____

ORCHID JOURNEY

NATURAL HABITAT

During your research, write down things like average rainfall per month, temperatures (daytime and nighttime), altitude, and any other information about this orchid's natural habitat.

ALTITUDE	AVERAGE DAYLIGHT (HOURS)

HUMIDITY

Country of Origin: _____

JANUARY	FEBRUARY
MARCH	APRIL
MAY	JUNE	JULY	AUGUST
SEPTEMBER	OCTOBER	NOVEMBER	DECEMBER

MAX TEMP

MIN TEMP

_____

222 - DENDROBIUM

ORCHID JOURNEY

Blooming Dates:

___/___/___
___/___/___

Dormancy Dates:

___/___/___
___/___/___

Type of Water Used

☐ Rain /Well Water
☐ Distilled
☐ Tap Water (pH _____)
☐ Other:_____

Preferred Fertilization Method

Humidity Preference

Temperature Preference

How Often to Water

Problems / Areas of Concern / Pests / Insects / Treatment:

_____
_____
_____
_____

Fragrant?
☐ Yes ☐ No

Rebloomer?
☐ Yes ☐ No

Likes / Dislikes

_____
_____

DENDROBIUM

ORCHID JOURNEY

LIFE CYCLE & FERTILIZER

Look for the key elements in fertilizer and adapt each fertilizing method to the appropriate stage. During the course of the year, cross off what you've tried. On the lines, write down what worked the best for this orchid.

K 19 Potassium 39.098

Calcium
Magnesium
Sulfur
Iron
Boron (Boric Acid)
Nitrogen
Potassium
Cooper
Zinc
Manganese

O 8 Oxygen 15.999

Seaweed
Tea Bags
Epsom Salt
Banana Peel
Eggshells
Other: _____
Other: _____
Other: _____

P 15 Phosphorus 30.974

Ca 20 Calcium 40.078

B 5 Boron 10.811

Mg 12 Magnesium 24.305

Stages of Life
- [ ] Root Growth
- [ ] Leaf Growth
- [ ] Dormancy
- [ ] Rebloom
- [ ] In Bloom

Date & Best Fertilizer

_____ _____
_____ _____
_____ _____
_____ _____
_____ _____

224 - DENDROBIUM

ORCHID JOURNEY

Awards?
- [ ] Yes   [ ] No

Which Awards:
_____
_____
_____
_____

What to Do Next (Action)
_____
_____

When to Do it (Time/Date)
_____
_____

Does this orchid have sentimental value? Why?
_____
_____
_____
_____

Spike Duration

Bud Duration

Bloom Duration

Numer of Blooms

Potting Medium
- [ ] Sphagnum Moss
- [ ] Orchid Bark
- [ ] Hydroponics
- [ ] Charcoal
- [ ] River Rock
- [ ] Other: _____
- [ ] Other: _____

[ ] Hybrid   [ ] Species

Parents (Cross):
_____
_____
_____

Candidate for Mounting?

DENDROBIUM

GENERAL NOTES

CYMBIDIUM

"A flower does not use words to announce its arrival to the world; it just blooms." – *Matshona Dhliwayo*

Cymbidium orchids are such precious jewels that they had to be included in this list. If you're wondering what a Cymbidium orchid looks like, the banner on Orchideria's website is a Cymbidium orchid.

Habitat, History & Identification

Cymbidiums are found growing naturally in the cool, bright areas near the foothills of the Himalayas. From there, they spread out over the cooler tropical and subtropical areas of Asia (covering the north part of India, and extending through China, Japan, Malaysia, Philippines, and Borneo) and finally reaching the coast of Australia.

These orchids are to be viewed differently form the tropical rainforest habitat; the environment we first think of when mentally visualizing orchids. At the bottom of the Himalayas, the climate is cooler yet still humid.

Since Cymbidiums are so common to these areas, 5 of the 55 species have been held in higher consideration. These 5 are the Asian Orchids, or the Chinese Orchids (yet they aren't exclusive to China.) The five Asian orchids are: Cymbidium ensifolium,

Cymbidium faberi, Cymbidium goeringii, Cymbidium kanran, and the Cymbidium sinense.

History of Cymbidiums

Cymbidiums are not a new plant to orchid growers. In fact, Cymbidiums are the oldest orchids grown indoors (or in greenhouses) that are mentioned. Their history across China dates back to Confucius (around 551 BC), when he mentions Cymbidiums, calling them the "Kings of Fragrance". They are also mentioned in writings dating back to the Chin dynasty, which is from 221 BC to 207 BC.

Yet, Cymbidiums weren't formally classified as orchids until 1799. A Swedish botanist named Olof Swartz (1750-1818) was the first to mention Cymbidiums. He called them little boats, in honor of the bowl-like structure of the bottom petal, (or the labellum).

Cymbidiums now had entered the formal documents of Europe and appeared in the first of Olof's six published books about botany, *Nova acta Regiae Societatis Scientiarum Upsaliensis*.

Why did Olof Swartz have the privilege of naming Cymbidiums? In other words, why was he so special? Swartz had a vast knowledge of botany and his personal travels to East Indies, Jamaica, and "the New World", as they called it, all built a solid base for this information.

Olof Swartz not only collected information; he was famous for his personal collection of over 6,000 orchids, which upon his death were donated to the Swedish Museum of Natural History. With his vast knowledge of orchids and his famous travels, he was offered a position with the East India Trading Company as a travelling physician on deck, but he refused it. Instead, Olof preferred to continue his studies in botany and venture out on his personal travels.

Meaning of The Word Cymbidium

Where did Olof Swartz come up with the word Cymbidium? Cymbidium is derived from Latin. **Cymba**, which means boat, cup or bowl was added to **-idium**, which means little. This perfectly describes the Cymbidium, since the bottom petal, called a lip (or labellum), looks like a small boat or bowl.

Cymbidiums became a fever in Europe after Olof Swartz made them known. One reason is long time that the flower can remain in bloom, which usually ranges from two to three months, depending on the species. The other reason is that they make an excellent cut flower for floral arrangements.

There are actually two distinct types of Cymbidiums, and their care is similar, so I'll include them in the same list. At the end of the chapter, I'll give a brief description of the second category and how they are distinct, but that really deserves a subchapter in itself (which, unfortunately, it didn't get in this book).

The main complaint that orchid growers have is that Cymbidiums will blossom once, and nevermore. This is because the conditions were met to some degree, but usually came up lacking in one area or another. In the Cymbidiums case, the culprit is usually a temperature drop at night.

Outdoor Light Requirements for Cymbidiums

Cymbidiums prefer high, bright light, but not direct sun. They don't like as much as Cattleyas or Vandas, which can tolerate direct sunlight, but are very close.

Place Cymbidiums on the outer edge of the shelf where light isn't as direct because even though they like light, they don't like heat. These are cool orchids, so the sun must never get too hot.

If you have your orchid outside, which it will absolutely love, then find a place where the light is bright, but diffused. A great place would be in the shadows of a filtered tree, where morning sun can reach it, but not more than that. Late afternoon sun could be stretching the light requirements to the top/maximum.

As long as the Cymbidium doesn't get direct sunlight for too many hours, has more shade than sun, and stays in bright light for the most part of the day, it will thrive in the outdoors. During spring to autumn, it will need more bright light than during winter.

Indoor Lighting For Cymbidiums

If you are growing Cymbidiums indoors, find the brightest windows in your house and place them there.

If you use artificial lighting, you'll need to not go over 5,000 fc (foot candles), which is the maximum tolerated. In this sense, Cymbidiums are right next to Brassia, Degarmoara, Dendrobium and Oncidium.

Fertilizer for Cymbidiums

You need to choose a balanced fertilizer every other week, which can be 20-20-20 or 10-10-10 and apply it from March to September. Once in bloom, which is late fall and winter, cut back on fertilizer to once a month. Some orchid growers prefer to use a 6-30-30 during the winter period, up until late February.

Since there are many different types of fertilizing methods, below is what the most common are for Cymbidiums. As you can see, some growers use 6-30-30 during winter. Once Spring comes in, start upgrading the Nitrogen, with a 30-10-10 or 20-10-20. In Summer, upgrade the Phosphorous, with a 10-30-20.

As you can also see with the graph below, just using a 20-20-20 year-round also works well.

During Winter Through February	**Spring to Late summer** During Root and Leaf Growth	**Summer** Boost spikes and buds for Fall
--	30-10-10 High Nitrogen (2x month)	10-30-20 High Phosphorus (2x month)
6-30-30 (1x month)	20-10-20 (2x month)	--
20-20-20 (1x month)	20-20-20 (1x month)	20-20-20 (1x month)

Water

Being native to the base of the Himalayas, Cymbidiums love humidity and cool water. Yet, they don't want to be wet all the time.

It's like taking a hike on a nature trail by a river. It's amazing to jump in and splash around in the water, but it's also fun to dry off with a towel later on. Don't stay in the river after dark.

Cymbidiums also don't want to stay wet after dark either. You'll need a small fan to promote air circulation, so the water inside the pot and around the stem will dry quickly.

Cymbidiums need the extra water. Unlike Phalaenopsis which need to have their root dry out in between watering, Cymbidiums prefer to have more water and not dry out. Yet they don't want to be soaked either. If you water your Phals once a week, water the Cymbidiums once every three days.

Watering Cymbidiums During Different Seasons

During the winter, you'll need to water less. If you keep up the same routine for watering, you will promote root rot. This happens because the water is absorbed by the velamen (a thin layer that protects the actual root) but since the orchid doesn't use the water, it just sits there…accumulating bad omens.

The root then suffocates and can't exchange oxygen and carbon dioxide. As it slowly decays, bacteria takes over destroying both the potting medium and the roots. So, in summary, don't water as much during winter as you would the rest of the year.

Temperature

Unlike most tropical orchids, Cymbidiums don't prefer the higher, hotter temperatures of tropical rainforests, and can better withstand the cooler nights. In fact, they love cooler temperatures. They tolerate even low temperatures almost down to a little above frost.

That being said, Cymbidiums are also outdoors plants. As soon as you can, take them outside. And that is strictly, as soon as you can.

They thrive well at anything above 58° F (14° C), but can still remain alive above 40° F (4° C) during the night. So as soon as spring rolls in, take your plant outside. Leave it there until the autumn nights drop to 40° F (4° C) again.

During the spring, summer, and fall, Cymbidiums should be outside in the shade. Verify the temperature where they are at is around 75° to 85° F (23° to 29° C) and that they are getting enough humidity. At night during summer, the temperature should be anywhere from 50 to 60° F (10° to 15° C).

If you're having problems getting the temperature to drop that many degrees at night, lightly mist the environment during the evening hours.

This is tricky advice, because you don't want to mist the leaves and have water droplets sit all night. This is a recipe for sure death. Make sure it's just a light misting, because just like the river at night, Cymbidiums will not do well if their leaves and roots are soggy and wet and night.

One of the main reasons that your Cymbidium will not bloom twice, is because the temperature at night is not falling enough. If you have your Cymbidium indoors, you'll need to turn off the heat at night, so it will feel the temperature difference.

This is true of most Cymbidiums. If you have a miniature Cymbidium, the night temperatures will not be as crucial to promoting blooms as the "non-miniature" plant would.

Humidity

Since your Cymbidium will be outside for a good part of the year, you won't need to worry about humidity (unless you live in a really dry area). If you think your orchid isn't getting enough humidity, you can try a humidity tray.

Once you bring your orchid inside during the winter, you'll need to keep it a little above normal indoor condition, anywhere from 40 to 60% of relative humidity (RH).

Since this is pretty high, always keep a fan on, even during the night hours. Air circulation will prevent root, stem, and crown rot, since the water will evaporate before it causes any harm to the cell structures.

Potting Medium

Being semi-terrestrial orchids, Cymbidiums need a potting mix that is both sturdy and will allow water to flow freely in and out of the pot. You can use a combination of different organic media that you'd like: osmunda fiber, fir bark, stones, sticks, perlite, charcoal, coconut fiber... The list is quite long.

When you purchase fir bark, aim for the medium grade as to the finer or larger pieces.

Since Cymbidiums like to be more moist than other orchids, adding sphagnum moss to the media will help to trap in that extra humidity that you're looking for.

Whatever combination you use, make sure water will flow quickly through the pot and not get trapped in between the various layers of media. If you want to avoid the hassle, you may use the same potting media that Paphiopedilums use.

But aren't paphiopedilum terrestrial? Isn't their mixture soil? Technically it's loam, a mixture of sand, silt, and clay. Cymbidiums can adapt to this medium because some Cymbidiums are terrestrial.

Make your Own Potting Media for Cymbidiums

It's hard to give one basic recipe for all Cymbidiums for the best potting medium, since seedling and older, larger plants will have drastically different needs. Where you live also will interfere in what should go into the potting media. If your climate is more humid, you can go with 40% large grade bark, 40% fine grade bark, and 20% perlite. If you live in a place that is prone to drier climates, you can change that recipe into a sandier media, which retains more water.

Repotting Cymbidiums

You need to repot in the spring, after the cymbidium has dropped its last blossom. If you repot while in blossom, you may lose the flowers, and bud blast or blossom blast may occur.

Cymbidiums absolutely detest being repotted, and will enter a phase of "draw back" until they get used to the new pot.

You might think that because the roots are protruding to the outside of the pot, that you need to repot. Actually, Cymbidiums are quite content being rootbound. It provides them with a sense of security and stability, so they can focus on producing blooms. This means you can keep your Cymbidium in its pot for 2 to 3 years before you repot, much longer than a Phalaenopsis.

If your Cymbidium is just way too big to fit in a pot and you need to divide it, count the pseudobulbs. Never leave a division of less than three.

Most Commons Pests

Since Cymbidiums grow outdoors most their lives, they will be more prone to outdoors pests, more so than other orchids. Snails, ants, wasps, slugs… If they're in your yard, they'll be in your Cymbidium plant.

But Cymbidiums also are more prone to viruses, especially the famous Virus Quartet: Cymbidium Mosaic Virus, Odontoglossum Ringspot Virus, Orchid Fleck Virus, and the Tobacco Mosaic Virus.

Cymbidiums are a great addition to your orchid collection, and so different form the orchids that are normally sold since they can easily grow outside.

CARE SHEET

Cymbidium

SPECIES	FOOT CANDLES (FC)
50 - 70	3,000 - 4,500

HUMIDITY
40 - 60 %

% SHADE	REPOT
20	3 YEARS

POTTING MIX
COARSE-GRADE

FERTILIZER	WATER PREFERENCE
30-10-10	WATER HEAVILY DURING GROWTH SEASON

DAYS BETWEEN WATERING	PH	FLOWERING
7-10 DAYS	5.5	1 x YEAR

MAX TEMP
75-85 F
23-29 C

MIN TEMP
>45 F
>7 C

GO-TO POTTING MEDIA FOR STARTERS

40% Small Grade Coconut Chips
20% Peat Moss
20% Perlite

For Dry Environments

40% Coconut Husks or Fir bark
40% Perlite
10% Charcoal
10% Wood Shavings

For Humid Environments

ORCHID JOURNEY

Cymbidiums

1 / 5

THE SEMI-TERRESTIAL ORCHID

ID/ Species | #

Date Purchased:

Place Purchased (Vendor):

Stage of Life When Purchased:

- [ ] Seedling / Flask
- [ ] Near Bloom
- [ ] In Bloom / Adult

First Impressions:
Leaf Size
Leaf Quantity
Roots
Number of Blooms

Light Intensity:

Orientations from Seller:
_____
_____
_____

First Repot:
(Root & Potting Medium)
_____
_____
_____

Last Time Repotted (Date)
____/____/____
____/____/____

238 - CYMBIDIUM

ORCHID JOURNEY

NATURAL HABITAT

During your research, write down things like average rainfall per month, temperatures (daytime and nighttime), altitude, and any other information about this orchid's natural habitat.

ALTITUDE	AVERAGE DAYLIGHT (HOURS)

HUMIDITY

Country of Origin: _____

JANUARY	FEBRUARY
MARCH	APRIL
MAY	JUNE	JULY	AUGUST
SEPTEMBER	OCTOBER	NOVEMBER	DECEMBER

MAX TEMP

MIN TEMP

CYMBIDIUM - 239

ORCHID JOURNEY

Blooming Dates:

____/____/____
____/____/____

Dormancy Dates:

____/____/____
____/____/____

Preferred Fertilization Method

Humidity Preference

Temperature Preference

How Often to Water

Type of Water Used
- [ ] Rain /Well Water
- [ ] Distilled
- [ ] Tap Water (pH _____)
- [ ] Other:_____

Problems / Areas of Concern / Pests / Insects / Treatment:
_____
_____
_____
_____

Fragrant?
- [ ] Yes [ ] No

Rebloomer?
- [ ] Yes [ ] No

Likes / Dislikes
_____
_____

- CYMBIDIUM

ORCHID JOURNEY

LIFE CYCLE & FERTILIZER

Look for the key elements in fertilizer and adapt each fertilizing method to the appropriate stage. During the course of the year, cross off what you've tried. On the lines, write down what worked the best for this orchid.

Calcium
Magnesium
Sulfur
Iron
Boron (Boric Acid)
Nitrogen
Potassium
Cooper
Zinc
Manganese

Seaweed
Tea Bags
Epsom Salt
Banana Peel
Eggshells
Other: _____
Other: _____
Other: _____

Stages of Life

- [ ] Root Growth
- [ ] Leaf Growth
- [ ] Dormancy
- [ ] Rebloom
- [ ] In Bloom

Date & Best Fertilizer

_____ _____
_____ _____
_____ _____
_____ _____
_____ _____

CYMBIDIUM

ORCHID JOURNEY

Awards?
- [ ] Yes
- [ ] No

Which Awards:
_____
_____
_____
_____

What to Do Next (Action)
_____
_____

When to Do it (Time/Date)
_____
_____

Does this orchid have sentimental value? Why?
_____
_____
_____
_____

- [ ] Hybrid   - [ ] Species

Parents (Cross):
_____
_____
_____
_____

Spike Duration

Bud Duration

Bloom Duration

Numer of Blooms

Potting Medium
- [ ] Sphagnum Moss
- [ ] Orchid Bark
- [ ] Hydroponics
- [ ] Charcoal
- [ ] River Rock
- [ ] Other: _____
- [ ] Other: _____

Candidate for Mounting?

GENERAL NOTES

Cymbidiums 2/5
THE SEMI-TERRESTIAL ORCHID

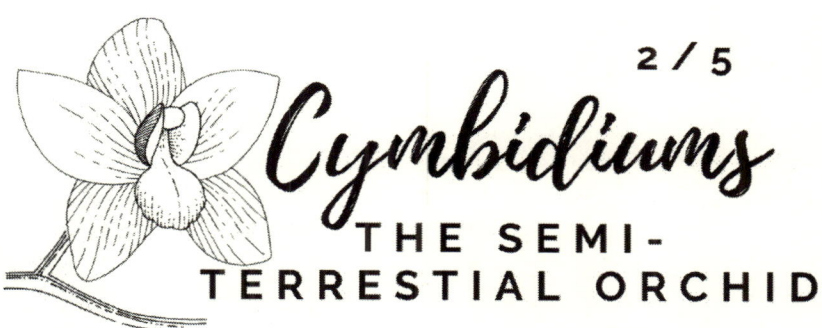

| ID/ Species | # |

Date Purchased:

Place Purchased (Vendor):

Stage of Life When Purchased:
- [ ] Seedling / Flask
- [ ] Near Bloom
- [ ] In Bloom / Adult

First Impressions:
Leaf Size
Leaf Quantity
Roots
Number of Blooms

Light Intensity:

Orientations from Seller:
_____
_____
_____

First Repot:
(Root & Potting Medium)
_____
_____
_____

Last Time Repotted (Date)

____/____/____
____/____/____

NATURAL HABITAT

During your research, write down things like average rainfall per month, temperatures (daytime and nighttime), altitude, and any other information about this orchid's natural habitat.

ALTITUDE	AVERAGE DAYLIGHT (HOURS)

HUMIDITY

Country of Origin:
_____

JANUARY	FEBRUARY
MARCH	APRIL
MAY	JUNE	JULY	AUGUST
SEPTEMBER	OCTOBER	NOVEMBER	DECEMBER

MAX TEMP

MIN TEMP

- CYMBIDIUM

ORCHID JOURNEY

Blooming Dates:

____/____/____

____/____/____

Dormancy Dates:

____/____/____

____/____/____

Type of Water Used

☐ Rain /Well Water

☐ Distilled

☐ Tap Water (pH _____)

☐ Other:_____

Preferred Fertilization Method

Humidity Preference

Temperature Preference

How Often to Water

Problems / Areas of Concern / Pests / Insects / Treatment:

_____
_____
_____
_____

Fragrant?
☐ Yes ☐ No

Rebloomer?
☐ Yes ☐ No

Likes / Dislikes

_____
_____

CYMBIDIUM - 247

ORCHID JOURNEY

LIFE CYCLE & FERTILIZER

Look for the key elements in fertilizer and adapt each fertilizing method to the appropriate stage. During the course of the year, cross off what you've tried. On the lines, write down what worked the best for this orchid.

Calcium
Magnesium
Sulfur
Iron
Boron (Boric Acid)
Nirtrogen
Potassium
Cooper
Zinc
Manganese

Seaweed
Tea Bags
Epsom Salt
Banana Peel
Eggshells
Other: _____
Other: _____
Other: _____

Stages of Life

☐ Root Growth
☐ Leaf Growth
☐ Dormancy
☐ Rebloom
☐ In Bloom

Date & Best Fertilizer

_____   _____
_____   _____
_____   _____
_____   _____
_____   _____

248 - CYMBIDIUM

ORCHID JOURNEY

Awards?
- [ ] Yes   - [ ] No

Which Awards:
_____
_____
_____

What to Do Next (Action)
_____
_____

When to Do it (Time/Date)
_____
_____

Does this orchid have sentimental value? Why?
_____
_____
_____
_____

- [ ] Hybrid   - [ ] Species

Parents (Cross):
_____
_____
_____

Spike Duration

Bud Duration

Bloom Duration

Numer of Blooms

Potting Medium
- [ ] Sphagnum Moss
- [ ] Orchid Bark
- [ ] Hydroponics
- [ ] Charcoal
- [ ] River Rock
- [ ] Other: _____
- [ ] Other: _____

Candidate for Mounting?

CYMBIDIUM - 249

GENERAL NOTES

3 / 5
Cymbidiums
THE SEMI-TERRESTIAL ORCHID

| ID/ Species | # |

Date Purchased:

Place Purchased (Vendor):

Stage of Life When Purchased:

- [ ] Seedling / Flask
- [ ] Near Bloom
- [ ] In Bloom / Adult

First Impressions:
Leaf Size
Leaf Quantity
Roots
Number of Blooms

Light Intensity:

Orientations from Seller:
_____
_____
_____

First Repot:
(Root & Potting Medium)
_____
_____
_____

Last Time Repotted (Date)

____/____/____
____/____/____

ORCHID JOURNEY

NATURAL HABITAT

During your research, write down things like average rainfall per month, temperatures (daytime and nighttime), altitude, and any other information about this orchid's natural habitat.

ALTITUDE	AVERAGE DAYLIGHT (HOURS)

HUMIDITY

Country of Origin: _____

JANUARY	FEBRUARY
MARCH	APRIL
MAY	JUNE	JULY	AUGUST
SEPTEMBER	OCTOBER	NOVEMBER	DECEMBER

MAX TEMP

MIN TEMP

252 - CYMBIDIUM

ORCHID JOURNEY

Blooming Dates:

____/____/____
____/____/____

Dormancy Dates:

____/____/____
____/____/____

Type of Water Used

☐ Rain /Well Water
☐ Distilled
☐ Tap Water (pH _____)
☐ Other:_____

Preferred Fertilization Method

Humidity Preference

Temperature Preference

How Often to Water

Problems / Areas of Concern / Pests / Insects / Treatment:

_____
_____
_____
_____

Fragrant?
☐ Yes ☐ No

Rebloomer?
☐ Yes ☐ No

Likes / Dislikes
_____
_____

CYMBIDIUM - 253

ORCHID JOURNEY

LIFE CYCLE & FERTILIZER

Look for the key elements in fertilizer and adapt each fertilizing method to the appropriate stage. During the course of the year, cross off what you've tried. On the lines, write down what worked the best for this orchid.

19 K Potassium 39.098

Calcium
Magnesium
Sulfur
Iron
Boron (Boric Acid)
Nirtrogen
Potassium
Cooper
Zinc
Manganese

8 O Oxygen 15.999

Seaweed
Tea Bags
Epsom Salt
Banana Peel
Eggshells
Other: _____
Other: _____
Other: _____

15 P Phosphorus 30.974

5 B Boron 10.811

20 Ca Calcium 40.078

12 Mg Magnesium 24.305

Stages of Life
☐ Root Growth
☐ Leaf Growth
☐ Dormancy
☐ Rebloom
☐ In Bloom

Date & Best Fertilizer
_____ _____
_____ _____
_____ _____
_____ _____
_____ _____

254 - CYMBIDIUM

ORCHID JOURNEY

Awards?
☐ Yes   ☐ No

Which Awards:
_____
_____
_____
_____

What to Do Next (Action)
_____
_____

When to Do it (Time/Date)
_____
_____

Does this orchid have sentimental value? Why?
_____
_____
_____
_____

☐ Hybrid   ☐ Species

Parents (Cross):
_____
_____
_____
_____

Spike Duration

Bud Duration

Bloom Duration

Numer of Blooms

Potting Medium
☐ Sphagnum Moss
☐ Orchid Bark
☐ Hydroponics
☐ Charcoal
☐ River Rock
☐ Other: _____
☐ Other: _____

Candidate for Mounting?

CYMBIDIUM - 255

GENERAL NOTES

Cymbidiums
THE SEMI-TERRESTIAL ORCHID

4 / 5

ID/ Species	#

Date Purchased:

Place Purchased (Vendor):

Stage of Life When Purchased:

- [ ] Seedling / Flask
- [ ] Near Bloom
- [ ] In Bloom / Adult

First Impressions:
Leaf Size
Leaf Quantity
Roots
Number of Blooms

Light Intensity:

Orientations from Seller:
_____
_____
_____

First Repot:
(Root & Potting Medium)
_____
_____
_____

Last Time Repotted (Date)

____/____/____
____/____/____

NATURAL HABITAT

During your research, write down things like average rainfall per month, temperatures (daytime and nighttime), altitude, and any other information about this orchid's natural habitat.

ALTITUDE	AVERAGE DAYLIGHT (HOURS)

HUMIDITY

Country of Origin:
_____

JANUARY	FEBRUARY
MARCH	APRIL
MAY	JUNE	JULY	AUGUST
SEPTEMBER	OCTOBER	NOVEMBER	DECEMBER

MAX TEMP

MIN TEMP

ORCHID JOURNEY

Blooming Dates:

___/___/___

___/___/___

Dormancy Dates:

___/___/___

___/___/___

Type of Water Used

☐ Rain /Well Water

☐ Distilled

☐ Tap Water (pH _____)

☐ Other:_____

Preferred Fertilization Method

Humidity Preference

Temperature Preference

How Often to Water

Problems / Areas of Concern / Pests / Insects / Treatment:

_____
_____
_____
_____

Fragrant?

☐ Yes ☐ No

Rebloomer?

☐ Yes ☐ No

Likes / Dislikes

_____
_____

CYMBIDIUM

ORCHID JOURNEY

LIFE CYCLE & FERTILIZER

Look for the key elements in fertilizer and adapt each fertilizing method to the appropriate stage. During the course of the year, cross off what you've tried. On the lines, write down what worked the best for this orchid.

Calcium
Magnesium
Sulfur
Iron
Boron (Boric Acid)
Nirtrogen
Potassium
Cooper
Zinc
Manganese

19 K Potassium 39.098

8 O Oxygen 15.999

Seaweed
Tea Bags
Epsom Salt
Banana Peel
Eggshells
Other: _____
Other: _____
Other: _____

15 P Phosphorus 30.974

5 B Boron 10.811

20 Ca Calcium 40.078

12 Mg Magnesium 24.305

Stages of Life

- [ ] Root Growth
- [ ] Leaf Growth
- [ ] Dormancy
- [ ] Rebloom
- [ ] In Bloom

Date & Best Fertilizer

_____ _____
_____ _____
_____ _____
_____ _____
_____ _____

- CYMBIDIUM

ORCHID JOURNEY

Awards?
☐ Yes ☐ No

Which Awards:
_____
_____
_____

What to Do Next (Action)
_____
_____

When to Do it (Time/Date)
_____
_____

Does this orchid have sentimental value? Why?
_____
_____
_____
_____

☐ Hybrid ☐ Species

Parents (Cross):
_____
_____
_____

Spike Duration

Bud Duration

Bloom Duration

Numer of Blooms

Potting Medium
☐ Sphagnum Moss
☐ Orchid Bark
☐ Hydroponics
☐ Charcoal
☐ River Rock
☐ Other: _____
☐ Other: _____

Candidate for Mounting?

CYMBIDIUM

GENERAL NOTES

Cymbidiums

5 / 5

THE SEMI-TERRESTIAL ORCHID

| ID/ Species | # |

Date Purchased:

Place Purchased (Vendor):

Stage of Life When Purchased:

- [ ] Seedling / Flask
- [ ] Near Bloom
- [ ] In Bloom / Adult

First Impressions:
Leaf Size
Leaf Quantity
Roots
Number of Blooms

Light Intensity:

Orientations from Seller:
_____
_____
_____

First Repot:
(Root & Potting Medium)
_____
_____
_____

Last Time Repotted (Date)

____/____/____

ORCHID JOURNEY

NATURAL HABITAT

During your research, write down things like average rainfall per month, temperatures (daytime and nighttime), altitude, and any other information about this orchid's natural habitat.

ALTITUDE		AVERAGE DAYLIGHT (HOURS)

HUMIDITY

Country of Origin: _____

JANUARY	FEBRUARY
MARCH	APRIL
MAY	JUNE	JULY	AUGUST
SEPTEMBER	OCTOBER	NOVEMBER	DECEMBER

MAX TEMP	_____
MIN TEMP	_____

ORCHID JOURNEY

Blooming Dates:

_____/_____/_____
_____/_____/_____

Dormancy Dates:

_____/_____/_____
_____/_____/_____

Type of Water Used

☐ Rain /Well Water
☐ Distilled
☐ Tap Water (pH _____)
☐ Other:_____

Preferred Fertilization Method

Humidity Preference

Temperature Preference

How Often to Water

Problems / Areas of Concern / Pests / Insects / Treatment:

_____
_____
_____
_____

Fragrant?
☐ Yes ☐ No

Rebloomer?
☐ Yes ☐ No

Likes / Dislikes

_____
_____

CYMBIDIUM

ORCHID JOURNEY

LIFE CYCLE & FERTILIZER

Look for the key elements in fertilizer and adapt each fertilizing method to the appropriate stage. During the course of the year, cross off what you've tried. On the lines, write down what worked the best for this orchid.

K 19 Potassium 39.098

O 8 Oxygen 15.999

P 15 Phosphorus 30.974

Calcium
Magnesium
Sulfur
Iron
Boron (Boric Acid)
Nirtrogen
Potassium
Cooper
Zinc
Manganese

Seaweed
Tea Bags
Epsom Salt
Banana Peel
Eggshells
Other: _____
Other: _____
Other: _____

B 5 Boron 10.811

Ca 20 Calcium 40.078

Mg 12 Magnesium 24.305

Stages of Life   **Date & Best Fertilizer**

☐ Root Growth   _____   _____

☐ Leaf Growth   _____   _____

☐ Dormancy   _____   _____

☐ Rebloom   _____   _____

☐ In Bloom   _____   _____

266 - CYMBIDIUM

ORCHID JOURNEY

Awards?
- [ ] Yes
- [ ] No

Which Awards:
_____
_____
_____
_____

What to Do Next (Action)
_____
_____

When to Do it (Time/Date)
_____
_____

Does this orchid have sentimental value? Why?
_____
_____
_____
_____

- [ ] Hybrid
- [ ] Species

Parents (Cross):
_____
_____
_____

Spike Duration

Bud Duration

Bloom Duration

Numer of Blooms

Potting Medium
- [ ] Sphagnum Moss
- [ ] Orchid Bark
- [ ] Hydroponics
- [ ] Charcoal
- [ ] River Rock
- [ ] Other: _____
- [ ] Other: _____

Candidate for Mounting?

GENERAL NOTES

MILTONIOPSIS

"Happiness held is the seed; Happiness shared is the flower." – *John Harrigan*

Miltoniopsis have had the fame of being a difficult, non-forgiving orchid, that will die on you if not given the exact conditions of its preference. They once were sold left and right, but now, given their bad name, they've dropped off the center-stage.

Miltoniopsis are not hard orchids to grow, but they have little tolerance of mistakes. That is why I've added them in the last position, coming in at 5th and not higher.

Just like any other orchid, they have their growing climates well-defined, and if you can meet them, you'll be rewarded will beautiful Miltoniopsis in flower for almost two full months at a time.

Most Miltoniopsis will rebloom after a few months, so you'll have them in bloom most of the year.

Characteristics

The first thing to know about Miltoniopsis is what orchid we are talking about. They are most commonly referred to as the Colombian orchid or the pansy orchid since they resemble the pansy flower in many ways. (Some say they resemble Oncidiums more than pansies.)

These amazing blossoms are extraordinarily huge compared to the plant and can display a waterfall pattern on their leaves, with white, yellow, red, orange, and peach colors. The blossoms are usually flat, with broad/wide lips.

They have long, thin, tender roots, which tend to be extremely fragile. These roots like to be in an always damp medium, where humidity is high and access to water is ever-present. There's a fine line from this to becoming soggy and prone to root rot, which is what usually happens to them.

The pseudobulbs will be longer, more elongated than their close relatives, the Miltonias, which are more circular. They shouldn't have wrinkled pseudobulbs, but flat and even. The shiny light green color indicates a healthy pseudobulb, with a smooth texture.

If the pseudobulbs are wrinkled, it's a sign that either there isn't enough water or the roots have problems and aren't absorbing the water that is provided. One or two spikes form from each pseudobulb, and four to seven pansy-shaped flowers emerge from each spike.

The inflorescence, most commonly called flower spikes, ranges from 8 to 20 inches long (20 to 50 cm). Some have reported them to blossom for almost two months, not quite that. I find that it's a bit shorter, ranging more in between five to six weeks.

Each flower, which is around 4 inches wide, or around 10 cm, will remain open for about a week and a half, and by the middle of the second month, they'll start to fall off. After a month or two of rest, they'll rebloom. This guarantees that the orchid will stay in bloom for most of the year, which makes the payoff worthwhile.

When not in bloom, the Miltoniopsis will largely assimilate resemble the Brassia, Odontoglossum and Oncidium orchids. Miltoniopsis was once a huge genus, but due to some pseudobulbs having two leaves, others having one; some being cooler gown and other withstanding hotter temperatures, the genus has been divided into Miltoniopsis and Miltonia.

The difference between the Miltonia and Miltoniopsis orchids

The main difference between the two groups is where they're found in nature. Because the Miltoniopsis grow in high altitudes, around the base of the Andes Mountain (mainly Colombia, Peru, Ecuador, and even in Costa Rica), and Miltonia are found in hotter, more arid climates, they have adapted to either retain more water or not—that's what distinguishes them apart.

Both orchid genus once were in the former, larger genus, commonly named "Miltonia". Later, Miltoniopsis were excluded (to form their own genus). The "opsis" suffix means pertaining to, or similar to.

According to Woody Carlson, author of the chapter "Culture of the Genus Miltoniopsis" published in Orchid Digest,

> "In 1837 John Lindley, a distinguished English botanist and orchidologist, established the Miltonia genus based on the warm-growing Brazilian species spectabilis (Lindl.), and dedicated it to the Earl Fitzwilliam, Viscount Milton (1786-1857)… In 1889 Godefroy-Lebeuf recognized that the Columbian-type species was structurally different from the Brazilian-type species and established the genus Miltoniopsis."

> It was only recently that the Miltoniopsis and Miltonia genus have in fact separated for good. "In 1976, Garay and Dunsterville reestablished the genus Miltoniopsis of Godefroy-Lebeuf for all the Columbian-type species of Miltonia."

Miltonias can only be found in the inland lower mountain ranges in Brazil, around the state of Minas Gerais. Having lived in Brazil for a good part of my adult life, these orchids are very familiar and in my biased opinion, easier to cultivate in our North American homes and offices than the Miltoniopsis.

Because Miltonias are not grown in such high altitudes and with considerably less humidity, they have adapted to warmer climates.

The differences don't stop there. Another variance between Miltoniopsis and Miltonias is that the pseudobulbs on Miltonias will have two leaves protruding from each pseudobulb, not just one. The round, circular-shaped Miltonia pseudobulbs will grow closer together, more compacted into the pot, as compared to the Miltoniopsis, which grow in the mountainous regions of the Andes, will be more elongated.

The cooler weather, found in Ecuador, Peru, Colombia, Costa Rica, and Venezuela will call for more humidity since Miltoniopsis like the foggy, humid, overcast rainforest of the tropics. Imagine a hike on a nature trail where hardly any sun will poke through the overhead leaves and it's so humid you can smell the sweet scent of approaching rain. In this habitat, it will rain every single day, and when it doesn't the humidity levels are approaching 90%. Miltoniopsis prefer this kind of weather—Miltonias don't.

Since it's a muggy, humid, but cooler climate, Miltoniopsis can afford to take up some space in the pot, and won't grow so close to each other. Each pseudobulb will prefer to distance itself from other pseudobulbs. They will spread out in the pot, having more distance on the rhizome in between pseudobulbs.

Warm-growing Miltonias, on the other hand, will grow crammed together, like childhood neighbors that know no limits to their friend's house and theirs. It's one big conglomeration of pseudobulbs inside a pot.

Basic Differences in Miltoniopsis and Miltonias

	Miltonias	**Miltoniopsis**
Native to	Brazil, Minas Gerais	High andes, Colombia, Pana, Equador, Costa Rica, Venezuela 500 to 2000 meters above sea level
Flower	Larger oncidium	
Temperature	Warm growers	Cool Growers
Leaf	2 leaves per pseudobulbs	1 leaf per pseudobulb
Pseudobulb	Round, Tightly clusters	Elongated, Spread out, long rhizome
Foliage	Gray-green	Yellow-green, mid-green

I've said this before, but it's a good time to repeat it. Miltoniopsis are not difficult to grow, though many consider them to NOT be a beginner orchid. I disagree. The main point to strengthen my argument is that to grow your Phalaenopsis (or any other beginner orchid) you had to read up on the culture, care, cultivation requirements, and the proper way to grow it at home. Without that information, you probably wouldn't have made it.

The same is true about the Miltoniopsis.

The only difference is that a Miltoniopsis will not be as forgiving as a true beginner orchid might be, as Phalaenopsis or Cattleya.

Buyer's tip: I hate to say this, but don't just purchase one. Buy three or four, because until you get the proper conditions that are suitable in your climate or indoors, a few will die on you. It's part of orchid care and learning.

So, don't take it as a negative experience if your first Miltoniopsis dies on you. Some do. Some don't. It can be that you did everything right and still it died. That's just part of orchid care and education. Everything is a learning experience.

Life cycle – when in bloom

Miltoniopsis run a strict calendar schedule and will bloom in spring. If you are in North America, spring will mean from April to July. Some Miltoniopsis will rebloom in the fall. Depending on the type of Miltoniopsis you have, (there are 6 known/registered species but hundreds of man-made hybrids) the inflorescence—flower spike—will emerge from the top or sides of the pseudobulb. Rarely will it emerge from both, but if it does, that it's not something to worry about. Consider yourself lucky.

The life cycle of a Miltoniopsis Orchid will be the following: During high, hotter temperatures, they tend to go dormant. This will usually be in summer. If your home environment is too hot, it may cut back the Miltoniopsis from blooming, since they don't tolerate higher temperatures. Keep them cooler and they'll thank you.

Once they have stopped their tiny dormancy period, Miltoniopsis will start to grow roots in late August and early September. (If you're not in North America, then read this as of late summer, early fall.)

You'll need to repot as soon as you see signs of new growth in the roots, but before the roots meet the old potting medium and start to bury. All your repotting needs to be done by October. If you missed it, then just wait a year.

On the downside, Miltoniopsis will not be forgiving in an old potting medium since they can't tolerate decomposing or decaying medium well, but that is preferred than trying to readjust a root that has made its way into the old medium.

The orchid has a new medium and is happily settled in its home. This should be October or November, signs of early winter. This is also the best time to purchase a Miltoniopsis. Order it online or get it from an orchid nursery, but buy it now. Don't wait until summer to buy it. This will give it plenty of time to adjust to your home environment and adapt before it's time to produce a flower spike. Too many changes and it will "shut down" on you. So...buy it, change the medium, and let it grow roots and healthy leaves during the winter, so it's ready to bloom in spring.

In spring, Miltoniopsis flourish to the fullest.

After their blooming period in spring, they might slow down a bit. It's not really a dormancy period but could be compared to one. In this case, you'll have flowers up to the end of summer, when it's time to repot (if you missed last year's repot) ...and that brings us to another year in the Miltoniopsis cycle of blossoming.

Light

Think back again to how Miltoniopsis grow in the forest. Imagine yourself walking on the uncharted path of a Peruvian rainforest, next to a waterfall with parrots and macaws flying overhead. Small micro monkeys are jumping from branch to branch, as bright, turquoise blue butterflies open and close their wings next to you. You can smell the humidity, and even though the sun is strong, it's not hitting you in the face. The leaves above from the tall forest make a closed canopy above you.

The sun rays that actually touch your skin are the bare minimum, (making you wonder why you ever wore sunscreen in the first place) even though it's bright enough to wear sunglasses. The sun isn't pouring down on your face but tiny light spots speckle the forest floor.

This is how much light your Miltoniopsis will need—next to none—but they'll like it bright. Don't push them off into a forgotten corner of your living room, waiting to rot away in blackness.

Considered low light orchids, Miltoniopsis are one of the few orchids that are good for bathrooms (and it's rare that I ever recommend an orchid for bathrooms) and the shelf furthest away from your light source if using LED Grow lights.

If you want a measurement, they range from 1,000 to 1,500-foot candles (fc), situated best with 1200 fc, which is very low. They are lower than the Phalaenopsis orchids. If you grow African violets, then mimic the same conditions to light as they like: shade, filtered light, and no direct sun.

There is a special note here: this applies to the cool growing Miltoniopsis. If you have the Miltonias, the genus from Brazil which is warm growing, you can increase the light level to 2000 foot-candles for warm growing.

Both are considered relatively shaded, but the Miltoniopsis is more, requiring 75% shade. Again, if you have a warmer growing one, then it will tolerate more light. Place a Miltoniopsis in more sun, and the tender, fine leaves will sunburn on you quicker than I will, when I forget to apply sunscreen.

Even late, afternoon sun that is fading into the evening shadows is too harsh for a Miltoniopsis. This means that if you have an east-facing window, that gets early morning sun no more than one hour, then the Miltoniopsis will appreciate it. Anything more than this, your orchid will struggle.

South-facing windows also don't work that well. The light isn't the problem here—the heat is. The south window is usually warmer and will stay warm all day long. Miltoniopsis are cool growing, and won't bloom is held in temperatures that are too high. (*Miltonias don't apply here.)

If you have grown or are growing a green leaf Paphiopedilum, then the light conditions would be the same. Miltoniopsis can take more light, if you drop the temperatures, so check the leaves to see if they are hot. If they are, it's too much.

Watering

Miltoniopsis grow in the humid, damp, overcast rainforest under the Andres Mountain range. They love water. If it's not raining there every day, the humidity is in the 90%, ready to downpour any minute. Then they dry out fast, caressed by the soothing wind currents that make the leaves in the overhead canopy play in the wind.

Since the Miltoniopsis leaves are thin, they don't have anywhere to store water. After all, why would they need to with it raining every day?

Miltoniopsis leaves aid in water evaporation. Any thin-leafed orchid will change the gas-exchange patterns, opening their stomata during the day instead of at night. If they'd absorb all the humidity in the air around them, they'd be quickly affected by edema—a swelling in the leaving provoked by overwatering.

During the day, humidity is already high so the stomata or air pores open to release the gases and extra water droplets without losing humidity.

Now take all that information and apply it to our home offices and living rooms. First, you'll need to water every day if you have a potting mix of orchid bark. If you use pure 100% sphagnum moss, then every five to six days should be sufficient.

During overcast days and cooler months of the year, you can hold back on watering. The plant won't work as hard to produce energy and require less water to live.

Note: If you have a warm-growing Miltonia, you can water less, leaving a few more days in between the watering periods.

Both Miltonias and Miltoniopsis are very intolerant to the salt build up in the medium. This means that you'll need to be flushing out the medium at least once a month, with water that is either rainwater, reverse osmosis water, or some other type of water that doesn't have as high a mineral count like tap water does.

Miltoniopsis prefer water with a pH of 6.5. Normal tap water is around 7.5 to 7.8, yet mine seems to range about 8.5 to 8.8. That's outrageously high, but that's another topic. Anything you can do to bring the pH down is highly appreciated by your plant—or just use reverse osmosis water, distilled water, rainwater, or some other cleaner form of water.

The excess minerals at the top of the medium (and consequently in the potting medium itself) need to be flushed out—this is a process named leaching. The salt build-up can happen because of the fertilizer, too. Once a month water normally, and after the watering, run clean water through the pot to rinse out any excess chemicals that have grown up inside your pot.

To know if you are watering a Miltoniopsis too little, the first signs will be wrinkled leaves and the second sign, a shriveled up pseudobulb. This may happen because the roots have all rotted away, so don't assume it's only because of underwatering. The leaves will have long pleats in them, like an accordion. This will not recover, even if you water every day. Once pleated, pleated for leaf life. You can recover the plant, but that leaf will always show signs that it's had a difficult season.

There is a popular saying with Miltoniopsis that if you think that they may need water tomorrow, water them today. But how do you know you need to water tomorrow? The roots are leaving their healthy green bean color and turning a silvery-white color.

You can check by the color of the roots, or by pushing your finger through a bottom third hole in the pot. Unlike the Phalaenopsis, where you can test using the top portion of the medium, the Miltoniopsis won't work with this method since you never want the pot to dry out extremely. Phals like to be a little dry every once in a while—Miltoniopsis don't.

If you feel the Miltoniopsis potting medium is wet, you still have to water it. That's why it's best to check the bottom holes on the pot. If they feel dry, then you've really underwatered the poor Miltoniopsis.

Temperature

These instructions apply to the cool-growing Miltoniopsis, since the warm-growing ones will have different, higher temperatures. During the day, you'll want to aim for no higher than 80° F (26° C) degrees. If you can keep it around or under 75° F (23° C), the orchid will appreciate it. Don't drop under 70° (21°C) for daytime. Above 80° (26° C), you're at risk for losing blooms or not even blossoming at all.

At night, you'll want to drop that temperature by 10° degrees, going no further cooler than 55° F. So, in summary, keep the temperatures from 55° to 65° F (12° to 18° C) at night and 70° to 80° (21° to 26° C) during the day.

Humidity

You need to do research on the internet, but be careful of who you read. I actually found this advice, "If well-watered, humidity is not a problem for Miltoniopsis." This is a pure, flat out lie. In my experience, there is no way ever that a Miltoniopsis will survive indoors without a humidifier. It's almost a tent-grown orchid, or greenhouse orchid because the humidity requirements are so high.

Think back to the rainforest under the Andes Mountains. They are in a high elevation climate, where the temperatures are cooler most the year. The humidity from the waterfalls, streams, constant and daily rainfall, and the bubbling brooks keep the humidity high, around 80 to 90%.

During the night, the levels will drop to around 50%, remaining higher at 80% during the day. If you don't want the constant changes, then you can successfully keep it at a 70% both day and night, and the results are about the same.

If you live in a hotter climate, then you'll need to upgrade your humidity, closer to 90%. The higher temperatures will open the stomata even more, and the gas exchange will occur more often, but this will also dry out your orchid more. More water will be absorbed through the roots, but also more humidity will be lost at higher temperatures.

Fertilizer

Miltoniopsis will need very little fertilizer, but regularly. The best solution for this is to dilute the fertilizer and use it every week, except once a month. On the day you don't fertilize it, you'll need to leach the orchid pot.

You can use less fertilizer during the winter months, or when it's very overcast and cloudy—almost the same routine as you would hold back the watering cycle. During blossoming time around spring, I recommend a 10-30-20 but during all other periods, a balanced on with high nitrogen is suggested, like 30-10-10.

Whatever fertilizer you use, dilute it much more than you would with a Phalaenopsis. A Cattleya and a Phal will forgive you for over-fertilizing, but a Miltoniopsis is a sentimental little dude and holds grudges. As we all know, grudges only harm the person that holds them, so your orchid will die from over-fertilizing and from excess salt build-up.

Very profound, I know...

But the physiological reasons are that the orchid is prone to be leached by nature every day and watering in abundance cleanses the excess nutrients out of the orchid roots. Miltoniopsis have thousands of fine, tender roots and collect tiny particles over a scattered period of time. Too much fertilizer and the plant goes overboard with chemicals, having no way to rid the excess.

The first sign that you're over-fertilizing is the blackened crusty tips at the end of the leaves. Cut the ends of these leaves off—they won't grow back or recover.

Tip: Miltoniopsis do not recover well from anything. That is why they have the fame of being non-forgiving. Any ailment that affects them will most likely kill them if not treated soon. Even root rot is hard to cure in a Miltoniopsis.

Soil – Media for Miltoniopsis

Since Miltoniopsis prefer to be soaked daily, yet depend on the air currents that sway through the trees, the potting medium needs to recreate these to the last drop. Any water retaining media with adequate drainage is what you'll be aiming for.

New Zealand Sphagnum moss is the perfect candidate for this. Not many orchids so well in sphagnum moss alone since it retains so much humidity. Seedlings can tolerate the constant humidity around the roots, which is what the Miltoniopsis like.

I had "technical" problems potting in sphagnum moss alone, so I kept around 20% orchid bark, just to say I had something else rather than sphagnum moss. I've had too many newly acquired orchids that came in sphagnum die on me... Too much humidity in the pot.

Since I usually get them on the promotion/sale table, they've had their death sentence written way before I even got ahold of them, but it still makes me turn my head against pure sphagnum as a potting medium.

Other orchid growers use it without restriction. This just reinforces that you have to try various potting mediums and see what works for you. Don't go blindly into what one person says, and that person only.

Miltoniopsis have been known to be potted in seedling bark, tree fern, and extremely fine orchid bark, too. There are other options, just keep the sphagnum more than 50% of your mix.

Without the sphagnum, your Miltoniopsis will dry too quickly.

Repotting

Since Miltoniopsis are epiphytes in a highly humid environment that get flushed out almost daily, they do not tolerate broken down potting medium. If you keep your orchid in the pot for more than two years without repotting it, it will die. The decomposing potting medium will hinder the quality of the absorption of the water through the roots.

When you repot, chose a pot that is the same size or near the same size as your actual pot. Miltoniopsis love to be root bound.

Since you'll have to repot next year anyway, it's not worth getting a pot 2 inches larger than the original, like you would for a Phalaenopsis or Cattleya. Keep to the same size and only upgrade when it's absolutely necessary.

As for mounting, the Miltonias will do better on mounts than the Miltoniopsis will. This is because of the warm-growing qualities: it's harder to keep a cooler environment on a slab than it is in a pot on your orchid shelf. Not sure why that is, but it's the way it is.

While your repotting, try to do this before the new roots actually touch the older potting medium. Once they have a taste of what the old potting medium is like, they will have a hard time adapting to the new medium. They grow roots very fast, so don't worry about not having good roots, as long as the new ones grow into good, fresh potting medium.

Grooming (Care after blooming)

You need to cut off the old flower spikes after the blooms have dried up and fallen off. Since the new growths that appear will be from a new inflorescence, you can cut off the old one without hesitation. If you absolutely want to, you can leave it on until it dries up.

This will provide some extra nutrients to the orchid, as it reabsorbs the nutrients it already has. Since it's not as thick as a Phalaenopsis spike and there isn't much to be absorbed, so I generally cut it off. There is no use keeping an ugly spike in the middle of something beautiful.

The second blooms will not last as long as the first since the months will be entering summer, and Miltoniopsis do not tolerate the hotter climates at all. The higher temperatures will stunt their growth, and the flowers will not remain open as long.

Tip: When you are cutting back the flower spike, be extra careful to not snip into the pseudobulb or other leaves. Miltoniopsis do not forgive cuts and scrapes so easily and this mark could become a hazard for future life.

Propagation

If and when you decide to divide your Miltoniopsis, make sure the division has at least 3-5 healthy pseudobulbs. Anything less than that will not make it. If possible, aim more towards five. The best time to do this is when you are repotting. You might lose the second inflorescence, but it's better to have a healthy potting medium for two years than to have a few sprays of flowers that won't last long in the first place.

Verify that the bulbs are in fact healthy before you divide them. If you happen to get a sick pseudobulb, chances are all the energy needed to survive will be transferred into trying to make the sick bulb recover. Miltoniopsis are not that hardy, compared to Cattleyas. You can make a whole bunch of mistakes on Cattleyas and if they get root rot, they just grow new roots. Not so with Miltoniopsis. These orchids are finicky in that aspect.

If your orchid is looking sickly, treat it immediately. Don't divide it, don't mess around too much with it, and let it heal. Chances are, once it's sick, it will not do so well... So, heads up on that. That is why we do everything in our power to avoid the sickness before it even installs in the orchid. Curing a sick Miltoniopsis is quite a job.

Don't pick an orchid pot that is too big, either. When you divide your orchid, remember that it probably won't grow as much that year. Since it does prefer to be rootbound, the orchid pot for Miltoniopsis can be tight, snugly hugging the roots.

Whatever you do, do not bury the pseudobulb into the medium. It should be above the medium and showing (visible).

Since your potting medium will be moist most the time, anything that is brushing up against it is a potential cause for stem rot.

Problems

Miltoniopsis are very prone to all the pests, insects, bugs, critters, and little creatures that should not inhabit the earth—but they do, and they're here to stay. Make sure you always verify the roots systemically for living critters.

The worst problem that Miltoniopsis have is the high humidity and constant water cycle leading to root rot. The roots are very fine, tender, and sensitive. It's not an easy task to get the cycle just right, but once you do, you're home free.

Cattleyas and Phalaenopsis are more forgiving when it comes to getting over root rot. With them, you can let the roots sit out, apply a bacteriacide, and the roots will grow back. Miltoniopsis are harder in that aspect. Even though they are avid growers, they don't recover well from diseases and have a hard time fighting it off.

Fungal infections hold a third place. This mainly happens because fungus feeds of bacteria, and if you didn't control the bacteria that caused the rot in the first place, it just adds up. Once fungus sets in, your potting media will decompose rapidly, and a repot will be necessary.

To treat both these, it's advised to keep a fan circulating at all times. The constant airflow will prevent water droplets from sitting too long on the top of leaves, in the crown, and next to the pseudobulbs. The air current dries up the water while making the available humidity circulate in between the orchid structures.

Hybrids – Varieties

There aren't many species of Miltoniopsis, only 5 (or 9, depending who you consult):
Miltonia anceps,
M. candida,
M. flavescens,
 M. cuneata,
M. spectabilis,
M. regnellii,
M. russelliana,
M. clowesii, and
M. kayasimae.

These have been crossed with each other and also with Vandas and Phalaenopsis to create hundreds of different hybrids.

When choosing a Miltoniopsis to purchase, always check and see who the parents are. This can influence minor adaptations in the culture and care guide.

CARE SHEET
Miltoniopsis

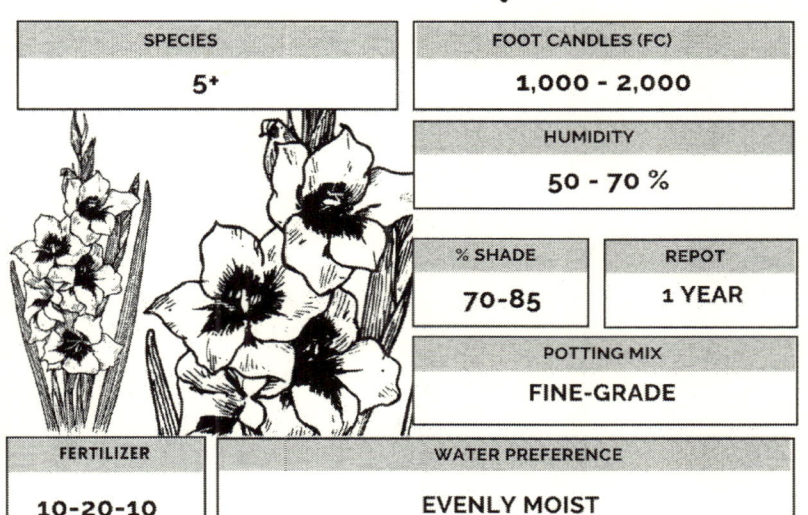

SPECIES	FOOT CANDLES (FC)
5+	1,000 - 2,000

HUMIDITY
50 - 70 %

% SHADE	REPOT
70-85	1 YEAR

POTTING MIX
FINE-GRADE

FERTILIZER	WATER PREFERENCE
10-20-10	EVENLY MOIST

DAYS BETWEEN WATERING	PH	FLOWERING
ALMOST DAILY	5.5-6.5	1-2 x YEAR

MAX TEMP
75-80F
23-26C

MIN TEMP
50 - 55 F
10 - 13 C

GO-TO POTTING MEDIA FOR STARTERS

PURE SPHAGNUM MOSS IS IDEAL, BUT TAKE YOUR WATERING SLOW. IF YOU USE THIS MEDIA, DO NOT WATER DAILY, BUT MIST DAILY.

IF PURE SPHAGNUM MOSS IS NOT YOUR PREFERENCE, MIX IT WITH BARK

ORCHID JOURNEY

Miltoniopsis 1 / 5

THE PANSY ORCHID

ID/ Species | #

Date Purchased:

Place Purchased (Vendor):

Stage of Life When Purchased:
- [ ] Seedling / Flask
- [ ] Near Bloom
- [ ] In Bloom / Adult

First Impressions:
Leaf Size
Leaf Quantity
Roots
Number of Blooms

Light Intensity:

Orientations from Seller:
_____
_____
_____

First Repot:
(Root & Potting Medium)
_____
_____
_____

Last Time Repotted (Date)

____/____/____
____/____/____

288 - MILTONIOPSIS

ORCHID JOURNEY

NATURAL HABITAT

During your research, write down things like average rainfall per month, temperatures (daytime and nighttime), altitude, and any other information about this orchid's natural habitat.

ALTITUDE	AVERAGE DAYLIGHT (HOURS)

	HUMIDITY

Country of Origin: _____

JANUARY	FEBRUARY
MARCH	APRIL
MAY	JUNE	JULY	AUGUST
SEPTEMBER	OCTOBER	NOVEMBER	DECEMBER

MAX TEMP	
MIN TEMP	

MILTONIOPSIS

ORCHID JOURNEY

Blooming Dates:

____/____/____

____/____/____

Dormancy Dates:

____/____/____

____/____/____

Type of Water Used

☐ Rain /Well Water

☐ Distilled

☐ Tap Water (pH _____)

☐ Other:_____

Preferred Fertilization Method

Humidity Preference

Temperature Preference

How Often to Water

Problems / Areas of Concern / Pests / Insects / Treatment:

_____
_____
_____
_____

Fragrant?
☐ Yes ☐ No

Rebloomer?
☐ Yes ☐ No

Likes / Dislikes

_____
_____

290 - MILTONIOPSIS

ORCHID JOURNEY

LIFE CYCLE & FERTILIZER

Look for the key elements in fertilizer and adapt each fertilizing method to the appropriate stage. During the course of the year, cross off what you've tried. On the lines, write down what worked the best for this orchid.

Calcium
Magnesium
Sulfur
Iron
Boron (Boric Acid)
Nitrogen
Potassium
Cooper
Zinc
Manganese

Seaweed
Tea Bags
Epsom Salt
Banana Peel
Eggshells
Other: _____
Other: _____
Other: _____

Stages of Life

- [ ] Root Growth
- [ ] Leaf Growth
- [ ] Dormancy
- [ ] Rebloom
- [ ] In Bloom

Date & Best Fertilizer

_____ _____
_____ _____
_____ _____
_____ _____
_____ _____

MILTONIOPSIS

ORCHID JOURNEY

Awards?
- [ ] Yes
- [ ] No

Which Awards:
_____
_____
_____
_____

What to Do Next (Action)
_____
_____

When to Do it (Time/Date)
_____
_____

Does this orchid have sentimental value? Why?
_____
_____
_____
_____

- [ ] Hybrid
- [ ] Species

Parents (Cross):
_____
_____
_____

Spike Duration

Bud Duration

Bloom Duration

Numer of Blooms

Potting Medium
- [ ] Sphagnum Moss
- [ ] Orchid Bark
- [ ] Hydroponics
- [ ] Charcoal
- [ ] River Rock
- [ ] Other: _____
- [ ] Other: _____

Candidate for Mounting?

292 - MILTONIOPSIS

GENERAL NOTES

2 / 5

Miltoniopsis
THE PANSY ORCHID

| ID/ Species | # |

Date Purchased:

Place Purchased (Vendor):

Stage of Life When Purchased:
- [ ] Seedling / Flask
- [ ] Near Bloom
- [ ] In Bloom / Adult

First Impressions:
Leaf Size
Leaf Quantity
Roots
Number of Blooms

Light Intensity:

Orientations from Seller:
_____
_____
_____

First Repot:
(Root & Potting Medium)
_____
_____
_____

Last Time Repotted (Date)

____/____/____
____/____/____

ORCHID JOURNEY

NATURAL HABITAT

During your research, write down things like average rainfall per month, temperatures (daytime and nighttime), altitude, and any other information about this orchid's natural habitat.

ALTITUDE	AVERAGE DAYLIGHT (HOURS)

HUMIDITY

Country of Origin: _____

JANUARY	FEBRUARY
MARCH	APRIL
MAY	JUNE
JULY	AUGUST
SEPTEMBER	OCTOBER
NOVEMBER	DECEMBER

MAX TEMP

MIN TEMP

296 - MILTONIOPSIS

ORCHID JOURNEY

Blooming Dates:

____/____/____

____/____/____

Dormancy Dates:

____/____/____

____/____/____

Type of Water Used

☐ Rain /Well Water
☐ Distilled
☐ Tap Water (pH _____)
☐ Other:_____

Preferred Fertilization Method

Humidity Preference

Temperature Preference

How Often to Water

Problems / Areas of Concern / Pests / Insects / Treatment:

_____
_____
_____
_____

Fragrant?
☐ Yes ☐ No

Rebloomer?
☐ Yes ☐ No

Likes / Dislikes
_____
_____

MILTONIOPSIS

ORCHID JOURNEY

LIFE CYCLE & FERTILIZER

Look for the key elements in fertilizer and adapt each fertilizing method to the appropriate stage. During the course of the year, cross off what you've tried. On the lines, write down what worked the best for this orchid.

Calcium
Magnesium
Sulfur
Iron
Boron (Boric Acid)
Nitrogen
Potassium
Cooper
Zinc
Manganese

Seaweed
Tea Bags
Epsom Salt
Banana Peel
Eggshells
Other: _____
Other: _____
Other: _____

Stages of Life
- [ ] Root Growth
- [ ] Leaf Growth
- [ ] Dormancy
- [ ] Rebloom
- [ ] In Bloom

Date & Best Fertilizer

_____ _____
_____ _____
_____ _____
_____ _____
_____ _____

298 - MILTONIOPSIS

ORCHID JOURNEY

Awards?
- [ ] Yes
- [ ] No

Which Awards:
_____
_____
_____
_____

What to Do Next (Action)
_____
_____

When to Do it (Time/Date)
_____
_____

Does this orchid have sentimental value? Why?
_____
_____
_____
_____

- [ ] Hybrid
- [ ] Species

Parents (Cross):
_____
_____
_____
_____

Spike Duration

Bud Duration

Bloom Duration

Numer of Blooms

Potting Medium
- [ ] Sphagnum Moss
- [ ] Orchid Bark
- [ ] Hydroponics
- [ ] Charcoal
- [ ] River Rock
- [ ] Other: _____
- [ ] Other: _____

Candidate for Mounting?

MILTONIOPSIS

GENERAL NOTES

Miltoniopsis 3 / 5
THE PANSY ORCHID

| ID/ Species | # |

Date Purchased:

Place Purchased (Vendor):

Stage of Life When Purchased:
- [ ] Seedling / Flask
- [ ] Near Bloom
- [ ] In Bloom / Adult

First Impressions:
Leaf Size
Leaf Quantity
Roots
Number of Blooms

Light Intensity:

Orientations from Seller:
_____
_____
_____

First Repot:
(Root & Potting Medium)
_____
_____
_____

Last Time Repotted (Date)

___/___/___
___/___/___

ORCHID JOURNEY

NATURAL HABITAT

During your research, write down things like average rainfall per month, temperatures (daytime and nighttime), altitude, and any other information about this orchid's natural habitat.

ALTITUDE	AVERAGE DAYLIGHT (HOURS)

	HUMIDITY

Country of Origin:
_____

JANUARY	FEBRUARY

MARCH	APRIL

MAY	JUNE	JULY	AUGUST

SEPTEMBER	OCTOBER	NOVEMBER	DECEMBER

MAX TEMP

MIN TEMP

_____
_____
_____
_____
_____

- MILTONIOPSIS

ORCHID JOURNEY

Blooming Dates:

____/____/____
____/____/____

Dormancy Dates:

____/____/____
____/____/____

Type of Water Used

☐ Rain /Well Water
☐ Distilled
☐ Tap Water (pH _____)
☐ Other:_____

Preferred Fertilization Method

Humidity Preference

Temperature Preference

How Often to Water

Problems / Areas of Concern / Pests / Insects / Treatment:

_____
_____
_____
_____

Fragrant?
☐ Yes ☐ No

Rebloomer?
☐ Yes ☐ No

Likes / Dislikes
_____
_____

ORCHID JOURNEY

LIFE CYCLE & FERTILIZER

Look for the key elements in fertilizer and adapt each fertilizing method to the appropriate stage. During the course of the year, cross off what you've tried. On the lines, write down what worked the best for this orchid.

Calcium
Magnesium
Sulfur
Iron
Boron (Boric Acid)
Nirtrogen
Potassium
Cooper
Zinc
Manganese

Seaweed
Tea Bags
Epsom Salt
Banana Peel
Eggshells
Other: _____
Other: _____
Other: _____

19 K Potassium 39.098
8 O Oxygen 15.999
15 P Phosphorus 30.974
20 Ca Calcium 40.078
5 B Boron 10.811
12 Mg Magnesium 24.305

Stages of Life | Date & Best Fertilizer

☐ Root Growth   _____ _____
☐ Leaf Growth   _____ _____
☐ Dormancy   _____ _____
☐ Rebloom   _____ _____
☐ In Bloom   _____ _____

304 - MILTONIOPSIS

ORCHID JOURNEY

Awards?
☐ Yes   ☐ No

Which Awards:
_____
_____
_____
_____

What to Do Next (Action)
_____
_____

When to Do it (Time/Date)
_____
_____

Does this orchid have sentimental value? Why?
_____
_____
_____
_____

☐ Hybrid   ☐ Species

Parents (Cross):
_____
_____
_____
_____

Spike Duration

Bud Duration

Bloom Duration

Numer of Blooms

Potting Medium
☐ Sphagnum Moss
☐ Orchid Bark
☐ Hydroponics
☐ Charcoal
☐ River Rock
☐ Other: _____
☐ Other: _____

Candidate for Mounting?

GENERAL NOTES

Miltoniopsis
THE PANSY ORCHID

4 / 5

| ID/ Species | # |

Date Purchased:

Place Purchased (Vendor):

Stage of Life When Purchased:
- [ ] Seedling / Flask
- [ ] Near Bloom
- [ ] In Bloom / Adult

First Impressions:
Leaf Size
Leaf Quantity
Roots
Number of Blooms

Light Intensity:

Orientations from Seller:
_____
_____
_____

First Repot:
(Root & Potting Medium)
_____
_____

Last Time Repotted (Date)

____/____/____
____/____/____

ORCHID JOURNEY

NATURAL HABITAT

During your research, write down things like average rainfall per month, temperatures (daytime and nighttime), altitude, and any other information about this orchid's natural habitat.

ALTITUDE	AVERAGE DAYLIGHT (HOURS)

HUMIDITY

JANUARY	FEBRUARY

MARCH	APRIL

Country of Origin: _____

MAY	JUNE	JULY	AUGUST

SEPTEMBER	OCTOBER	NOVEMBER	DECEMBER

MAX TEMP	
	_____

MIN TEMP	
	_____

308 - MILTONIOPSIS

ORCHID JOURNEY

Blooming Dates:

____/____/____

____/____/____

Dormancy Dates:

____/____/____

____/____/____

Type of Water Used

☐ Rain /Well Water
☐ Distilled
☐ Tap Water (pH _____)
☐ Other: _____

Preferred Fertilization Method

Humidity Preference

Temperature Preference

How Often to Water

Problems / Areas of Concern / Pests / Insects / Treatment:

_____
_____
_____
_____

Fragrant?
☐ Yes ☐ No

Rebloomer?
☐ Yes ☐ No

Likes / Dislikes
_____
_____

MILTONIOPSIS - 309

ORCHID JOURNEY

LIFE CYCLE & FERTILIZER

Look for the key elements in fertilizer and adapt each fertilizing method to the appropriate stage. During the course of the year, cross off what you've tried. On the lines, write down what worked the best for this orchid.

Calcium
Magnesium
Sulfur
Iron
Boron (Boric Acid)
Nirtrogen
Potassium
Cooper
Zinc
Manganese

Seaweed
Tea Bags
Epsom Salt
Banana Peel
Eggshells
Other: _____
Other: _____
Other: _____

Stages of Life

☐ Root Growth
☐ Leaf Growth
☐ Dormancy
☐ Rebloom
☐ In Bloom

Date & Best Fertilizer

_____ _____
_____ _____
_____ _____
_____ _____
_____ _____

- MILTONIOPSIS

ORCHID JOURNEY

Awards?
- [ ] Yes
- [ ] No

Which Awards:
_____
_____
_____
_____

What to Do Next (Action)
_____
_____
_____

When to Do it (Time/Date)
_____
_____

Does this orchid have sentimental value? Why?
_____
_____
_____
_____

- [ ] Hybrid   - [ ] Species

Parents (Cross):
_____
_____
_____

Spike Duration

Bud Duration

Bloom Duration

Numer of Blooms

Potting Medium
- [ ] Sphagnum Moss
- [ ] Orchid Bark
- [ ] Hydroponics
- [ ] Charcoal
- [ ] River Rock
- [ ] Other: _____
- [ ] Other: _____

Candidate for Mounting?

MILTONIOPSIS

GENERAL NOTES

Miltoniopsis
5 / 5
THE PANSY ORCHID

| ID/ Species | # |

Date Purchased:

Place Purchased (Vendor):

Stage of Life When Purchased:
- [ ] Seedling / Flask
- [ ] Near Bloom
- [ ] In Bloom / Adult

First Impressions:
Leaf Size
Leaf Quantity
Roots
Number of Blooms

Light Intensity:

Orientations from Seller:
_____
_____
_____

First Repot:
(Root & Potting Medium)
_____
_____
_____

Last Time Repotted (Date)

____/____/____

ORCHID JOURNEY

NATURAL HABITAT

During your research, write down things like average rainfall per month, temperatures (daytime and nighttime), altitude, and any other information about this orchid's natural habitat.

ALTITUDE	AVERAGE DAYLIGHT (HOURS)

HUMIDITY

Country of Origin: _____

JANUARY	FEBRUARY
MARCH	APRIL
MAY	JUNE	JULY	AUGUST
SEPTEMBER	OCTOBER	NOVEMBER	DECEMBER

MAX TEMP

MIN TEMP

314 - MILTONIOPSIS

ORCHID JOURNEY

Blooming Dates:

____/____/____
____/____/____

Dormancy Dates:

____/____/____
____/____/____

Type of Water Used

☐ Rain /Well Water
☐ Distilled
☐ Tap Water (pH _____)
☐ Other: _____

Preferred Fertilization Method

Humidity Preference

Temperature Preference

How Often to Water

Problems / Areas of Concern / Pests / Insects / Treatment:
_____
_____
_____
_____

Fragrant?
☐ Yes ☐ No

Rebloomer?
☐ Yes ☐ No

Likes / Dislikes
_____
_____

ORCHID JOURNEY

LIFE CYCLE & FERTILIZER

Look for the key elements in fertilizer and adapt each fertilizing method to the appropriate stage. During the course of the year, cross off what you've tried. On the lines, write down what worked the best for this orchid.

Calcium
Magnesium
Sulfur
Iron
Boron (Boric Acid)
Nirtrogen
Potassium
Cooper
Zinc
Manganese

Seaweed
Tea Bags
Epsom Salt
Banana Peel
Eggshells
Other: _____
Other: _____
Other: _____

Stages of Life

☐ Root Growth
☐ Leaf Growth
☐ Dormancy
☐ Rebloom
☐ In Bloom

Date & Best Fertilizer

_____ _____
_____ _____
_____ _____
_____ _____
_____ _____

- MILTONIOPSIS

ORCHID JOURNEY

Awards?
☐ Yes   ☐ No

Which Awards:
_____
_____
_____
_____

What to Do Next (Action)
_____
_____

When to Do it (Time/Date)
_____
_____

Does this orchid have sentimental value? Why?
_____
_____
_____
_____

☐ Hybrid   ☐ Species

Parents (Cross):
_____
_____
_____
_____

Spike Duration

Bud Duration

Bloom Duration

Numer of Blooms

Potting Medium
☐ Sphagnum Moss
☐ Orchid Bark
☐ Hydroponics
☐ Charcoal
☐ River Rock
☐ Other: _____
☐ Other: _____

Candidate for Mounting?

GENERAL NOTES

EXPLORING MORE

"A rose can never be a sunflower, and a sunflower can never be a rose. All flowers are beautiful in their own way, and that's like women too." – *Miranda Kerr*

Don't stop with only the orchids mentioned in this journal. This tracker was made so you can start your collection and keep moving forward. Not only your collection will expand, but also your knowledge on orchid care if you keep learning.

The following are 10 additional pages used to record places near you that might have orchid shows or expositions that you might be interested in.

Whenever you listen to podcasts, watch movies, read articles, and interact with others in your community, write that down. In time, this section becomes an easy reference to always look back upon.

ORCHID SHOWS

Name of Event: _____

Date: _____/_____/_____ Days: _____ Cost: _____

Location: _____ RSVP: ☐ ☐

Name of Speaker: _____

Notes: _____

Name of Event: _____

Date: _____/_____/_____ Days: _____ Cost: _____

Location: _____ RSVP: ☐ ☐

Name of Speaker: _____

Name of Event: _____

Date: _____/_____/_____ Days: _____ Cost: _____

Location: _____ RSVP: ☐ ☐

Name of Speaker: _____

Notes: _____

ORCHID SHOWS

Name of Event: _____

Date: _____/_____/_____ Days: _____ Cost: _____

Location: _____ RSVP: ☐ ☐

Name of Speaker: _____

Notes: _____

Name of Event: _____

Date: _____/_____/_____ Days: _____ Cost: _____

Location: _____ RSVP: ☐ ☐

Name of Speaker: _____

Name of Event: _____

Date: _____/_____/_____ Days: _____ Cost: _____

Location: _____ RSVP: ☐ ☐

Name of Speaker: _____

Notes: _____

ORCHID SHOWS

Name of Event: _____

Date: _____ / _____ / _____ Days: _____ Cost: _____

Location: _____ RSVP: ☐ ☐

Name of Speaker: _____

Notes: _____

Name of Event: _____

Date: _____ / _____ / _____ Days: _____ Cost: _____

Location: _____ RSVP: ☐ ☐

Name of Speaker: _____

Name of Event: _____

Date: _____ / _____ / _____ Days: _____ Cost: _____

Location: _____ RSVP: ☐ ☐

Name of Speaker: _____

Notes: _____

ORCHID SHOWS

Name of Event: _____

Date: _____/_____/_____ Days: _____ Cost: _____

Location: _____ RSVP: ☐ ☐

Name of Speaker: _____

Notes: _____

Name of Event: _____

Date: _____/_____/_____ Days: _____ Cost: _____

Location: _____ RSVP: ☐ ☐

Name of Speaker: _____

Name of Event: _____

Date: _____/_____/_____ Days: _____ Cost: _____

Location: _____ RSVP: ☐ ☐

Name of Speaker: _____

Notes: _____

ORCHID LITERATURE

☐ Magazine ☐ Video ☐ Podcast ☐ Website ☐ Association

Name: _____
Date: _____/_____/_____ Speaker/Author: _____
Topic/Main Focus: _____
Rating: ☆ ☆ ☆ ☆ ☆
Date and Time of Next Episodes/Volume:
_____/_____ _____:_____

☐ Magazine ☐ Video ☐ Podcast ☐ Website ☐ Association

Name: _____
Date: _____/_____/_____ Speaker/Author: _____
Topic/Main Focus: _____
Rating: ☆ ☆ ☆ ☆ ☆
Date and Time of Next Episodes/Volume:
_____/_____ _____:_____

☐ Magazine ☐ Video ☐ Podcast ☐ Website ☐ Association

Name: _____
Date: _____/_____/_____ Speaker/Author: _____
Topic/Main Focus: _____
Rating: ☆ ☆ ☆ ☆ ☆
Date and Time of Next Episodes/Volume:
_____/_____ _____:_____

ORCHID LITERATURE

☐ Magazine ☐ Video ☐ Podcast ☐ Website ☐ Association

Name: _____

Date: _____/_____/_____ Speaker/Author: _____

Topic/Main Focus: _____

Rating: ☆ ☆ ☆ ☆ ☆

Date and Time of Next Episodes/Volume:
_____/_____ _____:_____

☐ Magazine ☐ Video ☐ Podcast ☐ Website ☐ Association

Name: _____

Date: _____/_____/_____ Speaker/Author: _____

Topic/Main Focus: _____

Rating: ☆ ☆ ☆ ☆ ☆

Date and Time of Next Episodes/Volume:
_____/_____ _____:_____

☐ Magazine ☐ Video ☐ Podcast ☐ Website ☐ Association

Name: _____

Date: _____/_____/_____ Speaker/Author: _____

Topic/Main Focus: _____

Rating: ☆ ☆ ☆ ☆ ☆

Date and Time of Next Episodes/Volume:
_____/_____ _____:_____

ORCHID JOURNEY

ORCHID LITERATURE

☐ Magazine ☐ Video ☐ Podcast ☐ Website ☐ Association

Name: _____
Date: _____/_____/_____ Speaker/Author: _____
Topic/Main Focus: _____
Rating: ☆ ☆ ☆ ☆ ☆
Date and Time of Next Episodes/Volume:
_____/_____ _____:_____

☐ Magazine ☐ Video ☐ Podcast ☐ Website ☐ Association

Name: _____
Date: _____/_____/_____ Speaker/Author: _____
Topic/Main Focus: _____
Rating: ☆ ☆ ☆ ☆ ☆
Date and Time of Next Episodes/Volume:
_____/_____ _____:_____

☐ Magazine ☐ Video ☐ Podcast ☐ Website ☐ Association

Name: _____
Date: _____/_____/_____ Speaker/Author: _____
Topic/Main Focus: _____
Rating: ☆ ☆ ☆ ☆ ☆
Date and Time of Next Episodes/Volume:
_____/_____ _____:_____

ORCHID LITERATURE

☐ Magazine ☐ Video ☐ Podcast ☐ Website ☐ Association

Name: _____

Date: _____/_____/_____ Speaker/Author: _____

Topic/Main Focus: _____

Rating: ☆ ☆ ☆ ☆ ☆

Date and Time of Next Episodes/Volume:

_____/_____ _____:_____

☐ Magazine ☐ Video ☐ Podcast ☐ Website ☐ Association

Name: _____

Date: _____/_____/_____ Speaker/Author: _____

Topic/Main Focus: _____

Rating: ☆ ☆ ☆ ☆ ☆

Date and Time of Next Episodes/Volume:

_____/_____ _____:_____

☐ Magazine ☐ Video ☐ Podcast ☐ Website ☐ Association

Name: _____

Date: _____/_____/_____ Speaker/Author: _____

Topic/Main Focus: _____

Rating: ☆ ☆ ☆ ☆ ☆

Date and Time of Next Episodes/Volume:

_____/_____ _____:_____

ORCHID JOURNEY

ORCHID LITERATURE

☐ Magazine ☐ Video ☐ Podcast ☐ Website ☐ Association

Name: _____
Date: _____/_____/_____ Speaker/Author: _____
Topic/Main Focus: _____
Rating: ☆ ☆ ☆ ☆ ☆
Date and Time of Next Episodes/Volume:
_____/_____ _____:_____

☐ Magazine ☐ Video ☐ Podcast ☐ Website ☐ Association

Name: _____
Date: _____/_____/_____ Speaker/Author: _____
Topic/Main Focus: _____
Rating: ☆ ☆ ☆ ☆ ☆
Date and Time of Next Episodes/Volume:
_____/_____ _____:_____

☐ Magazine ☐ Video ☐ Podcast ☐ Website ☐ Association

Name: _____
Date: _____/_____/_____ Speaker/Author: _____
Topic/Main Focus: _____
Rating: ☆ ☆ ☆ ☆ ☆
Date and Time of Next Episodes/Volume:
_____/_____ _____:_____

- EXPLORING MORE

ORCHID JOURNEY

ORCHID LITERATURE

Magazine ☐   Video ☐   Podcast ☐   Website ☐   Association ☐
Name: _____
Date: ____/____/____   Speaker/Author: _____
Topic/Main Focus: _____
Rating: ☆☆☆☆☆
Date and Time of Next Episodes/Volume:
____/_____   _____:_____

Magazine ☐   Video ☐   Podcast ☐   Website ☐   Association ☐
Name: _____
Date: ____/____/____   Speaker/Author: _____
Topic/Main Focus: _____
Rating: ☆☆☆☆☆
Date and Time of Next Episodes/Volume:
____/_____   _____:_____

Magazine ☐   Video ☐   Podcast ☐   Website ☐   Association ☐
Name: _____
Date: ____/____/____   Speaker/Author: _____
Topic/Main Focus: _____
Rating: ☆☆☆☆☆
Date and Time of Next Episodes/Volume:
____/_____   _____:_____

ORCHID LITERATURE

Magazine ☐ Video ☐ Podcast ☐ Website ☐ Association ☐
Name: _____
Date: _____/_____/_____ Speaker/Author: _____
Topic/Main Focus: _____
Rating: ☆ ☆ ☆ ☆ ☆
Date and Time of Next Episodes/Volume:
_____/_____ _____:_____

Magazine ☐ Video ☐ Podcast ☐ Website ☐ Association ☐
Name: _____
Date: _____/_____/_____ Speaker/Author: _____
Topic/Main Focus: _____
Rating: ☆ ☆ ☆ ☆ ☆
Date and Time of Next Episodes/Volume:
_____/_____ _____:_____

Magazine ☐ Video ☐ Podcast ☐ Website ☐ Association ☐
Name: _____
Date: _____/_____/_____ Speaker/Author: _____
Topic/Main Focus: _____
Rating: ☆ ☆ ☆ ☆ ☆
Date and Time of Next Episodes/Volume:
_____/_____ _____:_____

EXTRA PAGES

It's impossible to keep just 5 of one genus. The addiction—passion—sets in and it's inevitable that you'll buy more orchids as time goes by. The next pages are for 3 extra orchids; 3 random note pages to fill as you wish.

ORCHID JOURNEY

Genus:

Notes: _____
_____
_____
_____
_____

ID/ Species | #

Date Purchased:

Place Purchased (Vendor):

Stage of Life When Purchased:
- [ ] Seedling / Flask
- [ ] Near Bloom
- [ ] In Bloom / Adult

First Impressions:
Leaf Size
Leaf Quantity
Roots
Number of Blooms

Light Intentsity:

Orientations from Seller:
_____
_____
_____
_____
_____

First Repot:
(Root & Potting Medium)
_____
_____

Last Time Repotted (Date)

____/____/____
____/____/____

- EXTRA PAGES

NATURAL HABITAT

During your research, write down things like average rainfall per month, temperatures (daytime and nighttime), altitude, and any other information about this orchid's natural habitat.

ALTITUDE		AVERAGE DAYLIGHT (HOURS)
		HUMIDITY

Country of Origin: _____

JANUARY	FEBRUARY
MARCH	APRIL
MAY	JUNE	JULY	AUGUST
SEPTEMBER	OCTOBER	NOVEMBER	DECEMBER

MAX TEMP

MIN TEMP

ORCHID JOURNEY

Blooming Dates:

____/____/____
____/____/____

Dormancy Dates:

____/____/____
____/____/____

Type of Water Used

☐ Rain /Well Water
☐ Distilled
☐ Tap Water (pH _____)
☐ Other:_____

Preferred Fertilization Method

Humidity Preference

Temperature Preference

How Often to Water

Problems / Areas of Concern / Pests / Insects / Treatment:
_____
_____
_____
_____

Fragrant?
☐ Yes ☐ No

Rebloomer?
☐ Yes ☐ No

Likes / Dislikes
_____
_____

ORCHID JOURNEY

LIFE CYCLE & FERTILIZER

Look for the key elements in fertilizer and adapt each fertilizing method to the appropriate stage. During the course of the year, cross off what you've tried. On the lines, write down what worked the best for this orchid.

Calcium
Magnesium
Sulfur
Iron
Boron (Boric Acid)
Nirtrogen
Potassium
Cooper
Zinc
Manganese

19 K Potassium 39.098
8 O Oxygen 15.999
20 Ca Calcium 40.078

Seaweed
Tea Bags
Epsom Salt
Banana Peel
Eggshells
Other: _____
Other: _____
Other: _____

15 P Phosphorus 30.974
5 B Boron 10.811
12 Mg Magnesium 24.305

Stages of Life
- ☐ Root Growth
- ☐ Leaf Growth
- ☐ Dormancy
- ☐ Rebloom
- ☐ In Bloom

Date & Best Fertilizer

_____ _____
_____ _____
_____ _____
_____ _____
_____ _____

EXTRA PAGES - 335

ORCHID JOURNEY

Awards?
☐ Yes   ☐ No

Which Awards:
_____
_____
_____

What to Do Next (Action)
_____
_____

When to Do it (Time/Date)
_____
_____

Does this orchid have sentimental value? Why?
_____
_____
_____
_____

☐ Hybrid   ☐ Species

Parents (Cross):
_____
_____
_____
_____

Spike Duration

Bud Duration

Bloom Duration

Numer of Blooms

Potting Medium
☐ Sphagnum Moss
☐ Orchid Bark
☐ Hydroponics
☐ Charcoal
☐ River Rock
☐ Other: _____
☐ Other: _____

Candidate for Mounting?

336 - EXTRA PAGES

GENERAL NOTES

ORCHID JOURNEY

Genus:

Notes: _____
_____
_____
_____
_____

| ID/ Species | # |

Date Purchased:

Place Purchased (Vendor):

Stage of Life When Purchased:
- ☐ Seedling / Flask
- ☐ Near Bloom
- ☐ In Bloom / Adult

First Impressions:
Leaf Size
Leaf Quantity
Roots
Number of Blooms

Light Intentsity:

Orientations from Seller:
_____
_____
_____
_____

First Repot:
(Root & Potting Medium)
_____
_____

Last Time Repotted (Date)

____/____/____
____/____/____

338 - EXTRA PAGES

NATURAL HABITAT

During your research, write down things like average rainfall per month, temperatures (daytime and nighttime), altitude, and any other information about this orchid's natural habitat.

ALTITUDE		AVERAGE DAYLIGHT (HOURS)

	HUMIDITY

Country of Origin: _____

JANUARY	FEBRUARY
MARCH	APRIL
MAY	JUNE
JULY	AUGUST
SEPTEMBER	OCTOBER
NOVEMBER	DECEMBER

MAX TEMP _____

MIN TEMP _____

ORCHID JOURNEY

Blooming Dates:

_____/_____/_____
_____/_____/_____

Dormancy Dates:

_____/_____/_____
_____/_____/_____

Preferred Fertilization Method

Humidity Preference

Temperature Preference

How Often to Water

Type of Water Used
- [ ] Rain / Well Water
- [ ] Distilled
- [ ] Tap Water (pH _____)
- [ ] Other:_____

Problems / Areas of Concern / Pests / Insects / Treatment:

_____
_____
_____
_____

Fragrant?
- [ ] Yes [ ] No

Rebloomer?
- [ ] Yes [ ] No

Likes / Dislikes

_____
_____

ORCHID JOURNEY

LIFE CYCLE & FERTILIZER

Look for the key elements in fertilizer and adapt each fertilizing method to the appropriate stage. During the course of the year, cross off what you've tried. On the lines, write down what worked the best for this orchid.

Calcium
Magnesium
Sulfur
Iron
Boron (Boric Acid)
Nitrogen
Potassium
Cooper
Zinc
Manganese

Seaweed
Tea Bags
Epsom Salt
Banana Peel
Eggshells
Other: _____
Other: _____
Other: _____

19 K Potassium 39.098
8 O Oxygen 15.999
15 P Phosphorus 30.974
20 Ca Calcium 40.078
5 B Boron 10.811
12 Mg Magnesium 24.305

Stages of Life

- [ ] Root Growth
- [ ] Leaf Growth
- [ ] Dormancy
- [ ] Rebloom
- [ ] In Bloom

Date & Best Fertilizer

_____ _____
_____ _____
_____ _____
_____ _____
_____ _____

EXTRA PAGES - 341

ORCHID JOURNEY

Awards?
- [ ] Yes
- [ ] No

Which Awards:
_____
_____
_____

What to Do Next (Action)
_____
_____

When to Do it (Time/Date)
_____
_____

Does this orchid have sentimental value? Why?
_____
_____
_____
_____

- [ ] Hybrid
- [ ] Species

Parents (Cross):
_____
_____
_____

Spike Duration

Bud Duration

Bloom Duration

Numer of Blooms

Potting Medium
- [ ] Sphagnum Moss
- [ ] Orchid Bark
- [ ] Hydroponics
- [ ] Charcoal
- [ ] River Rock
- [ ] Other: _____
- [ ] Other: _____

Candidate for Mounting?

GENERAL NOTES

Genus: _____

Notes: _____
_____
_____
_____
_____

| ID/ Species | # |

Date Purchased: _____

Place Purchased (Vendor): _____

Stage of Life When Purchased:

☐ Seedling / Flask

☐ Near Bloom

☐ In Bloom / Adult

First Impressions:
Leaf Size
Leaf Quantity
Roots
Number of Blooms

Light Intentsity: _____

Orientations from Seller:
_____
_____
_____
_____

First Repot:
(Root & Potting Medium)
_____
_____

Last Time Repotted (Date)

___/___/_____
___/___/_____

NATURAL HABITAT

During your research, write down things like average rainfall per month, temperatures (daytime and nighttime), altitude, and any other information about this orchid's natural habitat.

ALTITUDE	AVERAGE DAYLIGHT (HOURS)

HUMIDITY

Country of Origin: _____

JANUARY	FEBRUARY
MARCH	APRIL
MAY	JUNE	JULY	AUGUST
SEPTEMBER	OCTOBER	NOVEMBER	DECEMBER

MAX TEMP	
	_____
	_____
	_____

MIN TEMP	
	_____
	_____
	_____

ORCHID JOURNEY

Blooming Dates:

____/____/____
____/____/____

Dormancy Dates:

____/____/____
____/____/____

Type of Water Used

☐ Rain / Well Water
☐ Distilled
☐ Tap Water (pH _____)
☐ Other: _____

Preferred Fertilization Method

Humidity Preference

Temperature Preference

How Often to Water

Problems / Areas of Concern / Pests / Insects / Treatment:

_____
_____
_____
_____

Fragrant? ☐ Yes ☐ No

Rebloomer? ☐ Yes ☐ No

Likes / Dislikes

_____
_____

EXTRA PAGES - 347

ORCHID JOURNEY

LIFE CYCLE & FERTILIZER

Look for the key elements in fertilizer and adapt each fertilizing method to the appropriate stage. During the course of the year, cross off what you've tried. On the lines, write down what worked the best for this orchid.

19 K Potassium 39.098

Calcium
Magnesium
Sulfur
Iron
Boron (Boric Acid)
Nirtrogen
Potassium
Cooper
Zinc
Manganese

8 O Oxygen 15.999

Seaweed
Tea Bags
Epsom Salt
Banana Peel
Eggshells
Other: _____
Other: _____
Other: _____

15 P Phosphorus 30.974

5 B Boron 10.811

20 Ca Calcium 40.078

12 Mg Magnesium 24.305

Stages of Life
☐ Root Growth
☐ Leaf Growth
☐ Dormancy
☐ Rebloom
☐ In Bloom

Date & Best Fertilizer
_____ _____
_____ _____
_____ _____
_____ _____
_____ _____

348 - EXTRA PAGES

ORCHID JOURNEY

Awards?
☐ Yes ☐ No

Which Awards:
_____
_____
_____
_____

What to Do Next (Action)
_____
_____

When to Do it (Time/Date)
_____
_____

Does this orchid have sentimental value? Why?
_____
_____
_____
_____

☐ Hybrid ☐ Species

Parents (Cross):
_____
_____
_____
_____

| Spike Duration |
| Bud Duration |
| Bloom Duration |
| Numer of Blooms |

Potting Medium
☐ Sphagnum Moss
☐ Orchid Bark
☐ Hydroponics
☐ Charcoal
☐ River Rock
☐ Other: _____
☐ Other: _____

Candidate for Mounting?

GENERAL NOTES

ORCHID JOURNEY

Genus:

Notes: _____
_____
_____
_____
_____

ID/ Species | #

Date Purchased:

Place Purchased (Vendor):

Stage of Life When Purchased:

☐ Seedling / Flask

☐ Near Bloom

☐ In Bloom / Adult

First Impressions:
Leaf Size
Leaf Quantity
Roots
Number of Blooms

Light Intentsity:

Orientations from Seller:
_____
_____
_____
_____

First Repot:
(Root & Potting Medium)
_____
_____

Last Time Repotted (Date)

___/___/___
___/___/___

EXTRA PAGES - 351

ORCHID JOURNEY

NATURAL HABITAT

During your research, write down things like average rainfall per month, temperatures (daytime and nighttime), altitude, and any other information about this orchid's natural habitat.

ALTITUDE	AVERAGE DAYLIGHT (HOURS)

HUMIDITY

Country of Origin: _____

JANUARY	FEBRUARY

MARCH	APRIL

MAY	JUNE	JULY	AUGUST

SEPTEMBER	OCTOBER	NOVEMBER	DECEMBER

MAX TEMP

MIN TEMP

352 - EXTRA PAGES

ORCHID JOURNEY

Blooming Dates:

____/____/____

____/____/____

Dormancy Dates:

____/____/____

____/____/____

Type of Water Used

☐ Rain /Well Water
☐ Distilled
☐ Tap Water (pH _____)
☐ Other: _____

Preferred Fertilization Method

Humidity Preference

Temperature Preference

How Often to Water

Problems / Areas of Concern / Pests / Insects / Treatment:
_____
_____
_____
_____

Fragrant?
☐ Yes ☐ No

Rebloomer?
☐ Yes ☐ No

Likes / Dislikes
_____
_____

ORCHID JOURNEY

LIFE CYCLE & FERTILIZER

Look for the key elements in fertilizer and adapt each fertilizing method to the appropriate stage. During the course of the year, cross off what you've tried. On the lines, write down what worked the best for this orchid.

Calcium
Magnesium
Sulfur
Iron
Boron (Boric Acid)
Nirtrogen
Potassium
Cooper
Zinc
Manganese

Seaweed
Tea Bags
Epsom Salt
Banana Peel
Eggshells
Other: _____
Other: _____
Other: _____

Stages of Life

☐ Root Growth
☐ Leaf Growth
☐ Dormancy
☐ Rebloom
☐ In Bloom

Date & Best Fertilizer

_____ _____
_____ _____
_____ _____
_____ _____
_____ _____

354 - EXTRA PAGES

ORCHID JOURNEY

Awards?
☐ Yes   ☐ No

Which Awards:
_____
_____
_____
_____

What to Do Next (Action)
_____
_____

When to Do it (Time/Date)
_____
_____

Does this orchid have sentimental value? Why?
_____
_____
_____
_____

☐ Hybrid   ☐ Species

Parents (Cross):
_____
_____
_____

Spike Duration

Bud Duration

Bloom Duration

Numer of Blooms

Potting Medium
☐ Sphagnum Moss
☐ Orchid Bark
☐ Hydroponics
☐ Charcoal
☐ River Rock
☐ Other: _____
☐ Other: _____

Candidate for Mounting?

EXTRA PAGES

GENERAL NOTES

About the Author

Hi, there. I'm Amanda Matthews. It's a pleasure to meet you! If you're wondering who wrote this book, here's a little excerpt about me.

My parents were overseas missionaries, so I've had the privilege to travel with them to Kenya, Zimbabwe, Egypt, and Israel. We were stationed in Brazil for the majority of my life. Although I'm American, I consider myself a child of several nationalities.

After receiving a Masters of Divinity in Theology, I went back to Brazil and worked with the underprivileged children in the suburbs.

Drug addiction, adolescent pregnancy, abortions, school dropouts, unresolved family relationships, and substance abuse were common.

I know... you're wondering where do orchids fit in the conglomerate here... I'm getting to it. :)

Heart-wrenching fact: 1 in 5 women are murdered everyday by their husbands in Brazil. To understand them more, I specialized in the Theology of Comparative Religion and became a women's pastor dealing with topics of marriage, divorce, and abuse.

Little did I know, I had married an abusive and manipulative partner myself. My husband had grown in the military ranks and was now the highest-ranking colonel in the Brazilian military. The violence and danger came to a level I could not bear anymore.

Fearing for my life, I said a prayer, packed a suitcase, and fled in the middle of the night with my two small children. I only had $ 250.00 dollars in my purse and half a tank of gas. I lived off the grid for three years, not knowing where my next meal would be our how I'd cross 5,000 miles of land to get back home to Kansas. Needless to say, God brought me back safely with my two children.

I narrated that emotion-filled, gut-wrenching story into a memoir, titled Shattered Sanctuary. It is available on Amazon.

Fast forwarding to the present day... Now I dedicate my time to help others find the courage and strength to walk away from the hurt and build a new life. I'm a theologian, a pastor, and a motivational speaker, focusing on overcoming obstacles and rebuilding your life after toxic relationships. My main goal is to bring people closer to God.

What does all this have to do with orchids?

Finally, the whole point of why I had the idea to build a website, make a YouTube Channel, and write this book... Once I moved back home to the USA after living most my life in tropical sun-filled climates, I had a hard time making it through the horrendous winter in Kansas.

Accustomed to living in 60-to-80-degree weather year-round with long sunny days, I didn't adapt too well with almost 6 months of cold weather and dark, short days.

Since I couldn't return to Brazil, I either could bring nature inside my home by recreating those tropical surroundings, or move to Hong Kong (the weather is similar to Brazil's.) After failing miserably in my three-minute Mandarin lesson, I pulled up my big-girl britches and faced the Kansas winters.

Kansas adaptation it is.

I hadn't realized how much I missed being around orchids, which was a natural thing in Brazil. They were attached to every tree I owned in my house there. The major difference is that God did the watering, fertilization, and light requirements... I had nothing to do with their growth.

In addition to helping me with seasonal depression, working with orchids gave me a sense of peace and fulfillment. I'm naturally a teacher, a theological professor, and love to share what I know. I certainly don't have all the answers since I've had to relearn how to grow these amazing plants in a totally new environment.

I'm not an expert. I've sadly killed many orchids in the process of trying to bring such an exotic plant into my dry and sun-deprived living-room. This didn't help my depression, either.

I spent hours online, in the library (yes, I'm old fashioned and still go to those...LOL), and doing courses, investing in books, tutorials, and webinars, all to try to relearn what I once took for granted.

My initial question was: How in the world can I grow an orchid in Kansas? Literally thousands of hours of research went into to making my living room a natural habitat just so my small orchid plants would survive. It was my way of surviving winter.

The initial knowledge led me to share what I know on the website www.orchideria.com. I still get a lot of things wrong, and that is why I love the community, where we can exchange information and learn together. That is why I encourage the comments and interaction.

Unrelated information about me: when I'm not working on my next theological book, I'm out hiking on a nature trail, exploring waterfalls, or inventing new recipes to barbecue on the grill with my children.

I'm in love with this new phase of my life.

Googling new places to camp out has become my expertise while I hear the crackling of the fireplace. The only negative sound I hear is my alarm clock persuading me to get up and face my morning jog. But that one, I don't mind at all.

~Amanda June Matthews.

The End... Wait, There's More!

If this journal has helped in any way, I'd appreciate it if you left a review explaining what you thought of it. It really helps me out as the creator of this journal to understand what you'd like changed or modified, or if you'd keep it the way it is.

I'd like to make this journal one that will fulfill your needs while you're just starting out.

Without knowing what you'd like to add or delete, I can't make this into better versions in the future. For this reason, I'd really appreciate your review and will be looking forward to improving this journal in future editions.

Back to The Beginning

In the very first pages of this book, I mentioned the idea of an excel spreadsheet. The truth is that this book, being physically limited by page number, will last you a year, maybe 2. If you have over 30 orchids, then this book already doesn't fit your needs. Sooner or later, you'll need to move to a spreadsheet.

Guess what? **I'm already working on a way to download these sheets into a printable file.** It's currently in progress and as soon as it's done, you'll be able to download it for free at **www.orchideria.com.**

This is my way of saying, "Thank you for being a part of this community at Orchideria." I wish you all the best in your orchid care.

Happy cultivating!

Made in the USA
Middletown, DE
26 May 2022